WARNING:

While National Geographic has worked to make sure that the following survival tips and tricks come from the most accurate and up-to-date sources, you should know that sharks and lions could care less about what's written in here. Tornadoes and avalanches don't follow directions. And boats will pretty much drift wherever they want.

Translation? No matter how careful you are, no matter how many rules you follow, bad stuff can happen. So even though this book is packed with advice from the experts, such advice isn't always guaranteed to work.

(Now for the grownup legalese: All content and information published in this book is provided to the reader "as is" and without any warranties. The situations and activities described in the book carry inherent risks and hazards. The reader must evaluate and bear all risks associated with use of the information provided in this book, including those risks associated with reliance on the accuracy, thoroughness, utility, or appropriateness of the information for any particular situation. The authors and publisher specifically disclaim all responsibility for any liability, loss, or risk personal or otherwise, which is incurred as a consequence of the use or application of any of the contents in this book.)

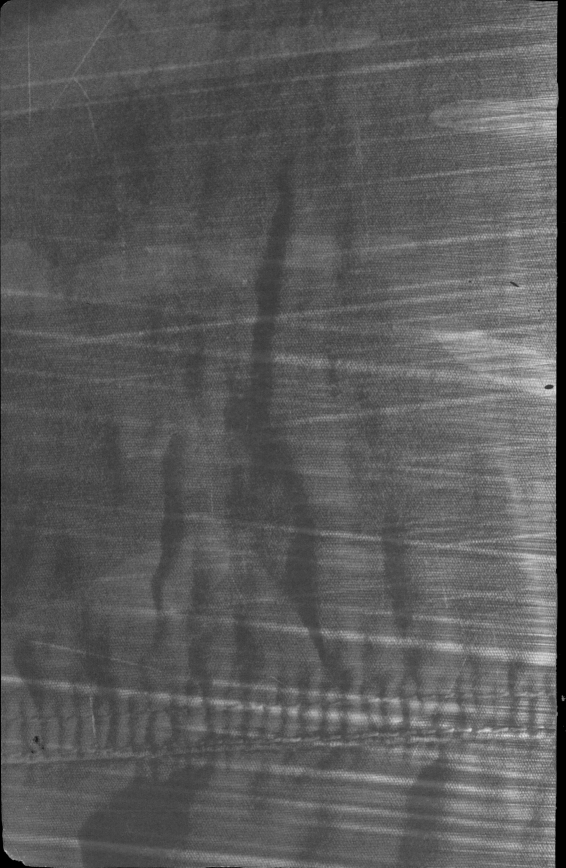

NAT GEO

HOW TO SURVIVE ANYTHING

BY RACHEL BUCHHOLZ

ILLUSTRATIONS BY CHRIS PHILPOT

NATIONAL GEOGRAPHIC
WASHINGTON, D.C.

To Joe, who somehow survives life with me every day.

To Dad, who needs only his smile to survive.

To Mom, a true survivor.

The National Geographic Society is one of the world's largest nonprofit scientific and educational organizations. Founded in 1888 to "increase and diffuse geographic knowledge," the Society works to inspire people to care about the planet. National Geographic reflects the world through its magazines, television programs, films, music and radio, books, DVDs, maps, exhibitions, live events, school publishing programs, interactive media and merchandise. National Geographic magazine, the Society's official journal, published in English and 32 local-language editions, is read by more than 35 million people each month. The National Geographic Channel reaches 310 million households in 34 languages in 165 countries. National Geographic Digital Media receives more than 13 million visitors a month. National Geographic has funded more than 9,200 scientific research, conservation and exploration projects and supports an education program promoting geography literacy. For more information, visit nationalgeographic.com.

For more information, please call 1-800-NGS LINE (647-5463) or write to the following address:
National Geographic Society
1145 17th Street N.W.
Washington, D.C. 20036-4688 U.S.A.

Visit us online at
www.nationalgeographic.com/books

For librarians and teachers:
www.ngchildrensbooks.org

More for kids from National Geographic:
kids.nationalgeographic.com

For information about special discounts for bulk purchases, please contact National Geographic Books Special Sales:
ngspecsales@ngs.org

For rights or permissions inquiries, please contact National Geographic Books Subsidiary Rights:
ngbookrights@ngs.org

© Copyright 2011
National Geographic Society

Library of Congress Cataloging-in-Publication Data

Buchholz, Rachel.
 How to survive anything : shark attack, lightning, embarrassing parents, pop quizzes, and other perilous situations / by Rachel Buchholz.
   p. cm.
 ISBN 978-1-4263-0774-4 (pbk. : alk. paper)
 1. Survival skills. 2. Life skills. I. Title.
 GF86.B83 2011
 646.7--dc22

2010028045

PHOTO CREDITS:
8-9, OTIS IMBODEN/ NATIONALGEOGRAPHICSTOCK.COM; 13 (TOP), LUIS MARDEN/ NATIONALGEOGRAPHICSTOCK.COM; 13 (BOTTOM), GALYNA ANDRUSHKO/ SHUTTERSTOCK; 21, ANDRESR/ SHUTTERSTOCK; 22-23, OAR/ ERL/ NATIONAL SEVERE STORMS LABORATORY/ NOAA; 27 (LEFT), TRAVIS MANLEY/ SHUTTERSTOCK; 27 (CENTER), GERT JOHANNES JACOBUS VREY/ SHUTTERSTOCK; 27 (RIGHT), TATNIZ/ SHUTTERSTOCK; 31, DANIEL BRIM/ YOUR SHOT/ NATIONALGEOGRAPHICSTOCK.COM; 41, BILL ELLZAY/ NATIONALGEOGRAPHICSTOCK.COM; 47, SCOTT KLEINMAN/ PHOTODISC/ GETTY IMAGES; 51 (BOTTOM), GUO JIAN SHE / REDLINK/ REDLINK/ CORBIS; 56, BETTMANN/ CORBIS; 57 (TOP), MICHAEL TRAN/ FILMMAGIC/ GETTY IMAGES; 57 (BOTTOM), KEVIN REECE/ICON SMI/ CORBIS; 61 (TOP LEFT), IVAN PONOMAREV/ SHUTTERSTOCK; 61 (TOP RIGHT), FOTOMAK/ SHUTTERSTOCK; 61 (BOTTOM), DIGITAL VISION; 62 (TOP), MASA-AKI HORIMACHI/ AFLO RELAX/ CORBIS; 62 (BOTTOM), OTIS IMBODEN/ NATIONALGEOGRAPHICSTOCK.COM; 63, NASA/ NATIONALGEOGRAPHICSTOCK.COM; 64-65, DAVID DOUBILET/ NATIONALGEOGRAPHICSTOCK.COM; 69 (TOP), R. MARTENS/ SHUTTERSTOCK; 69 (BOTTOM), S.R. MAGLIONE/ SHUTTERSTOCK; 79, ISLAND EFFECTS/ ISTOCKPHOTO.COM; 80 (TOP), DIGITAL VISION/ GETTY IMAGES; 80 (CENTER), IAN SCOTT/ SHUTTERSTOCK; 80 (BOTTOM), A COTTON PHOTO/ SHUTTERSTOCK; 81 (TOP), FIONA AYERST/ SHUTTERSTOCK; 81 (BOTTOM), DAVID DOUBILET/ NATIONALGEOGRAPHICSTOCK.COM; 89, MARTIN HARVEY/ CORBIS; 90 (TOP), VINCENT GRAFHORST/ FOTO NATURA/ MINDEN PICTURES; 90 (BOTTOM), BMCL/ SHUTTERSTOCK; 91 (TOP), MICHAEL & PATRICIA FOGDEN/ MINDEN PICTURES; 91 (BOTTOM), CHRIS JOHNS/ NATIONALGEOGRAPHICSTOCK.COM; 99, ANDRÉ GONÇALVES/ SHUTTERSTOCK; 100, AUDREY SNIDER-BELL/ SHUTTERSTOCK; 101 (TOP), JAMES VAN DEN BROEK/ SHUTTERSTOCK; 101 (BOTTOM), DMITRIJS BINDEMANIS/ SHUTTERSTOCK; 111, BRAD TALBOTT, LITTLE PLANET LEARNING, INC.; 112 (TOP LEFT), MOGENS TROLLE/ SHUTTERSTOCK; 112 (TOP RIGHT), LORI EPSTEIN/ WWW.LORIEPSTEIN.COM; 112 (BOTTOM), STEVEN GIBSON/ SHUTTERSTOCK; 114-115, JAMES P. BLAIR/ NATIONALGEOGRAPHICSTOCK.COM; 140, PHISEKSIT/ SHUTTERSTOCK; 156 (LEFT), OBJECTSFORALL/ SHUTTERSTOCK; 156 (RIGHT), YUVIS STUDIO/ SHUTTERSTOCK; 168, DIGITAL VISION; 169, ARNOLD JOHN LABRENTZ/ SHUTTERSTOCK

Printed in China
11/RRDS/1

IT'S ROUGH OUT THERE:

Sharks are circling, and you have no idea what else is lurking nearby. It's so easy to feel totally lost, or like a wildfire is raging and you can't breathe. You're seriously wondering if there's any way you're gonna survive.

And that's just school.

Welcome to your life, where it seems like an avalanche of homework can bury you just as quickly as an avalanche of snow, and your first day of school might feel a little like crashing on a desert island—you're alone, lost, and sweating way too much. One day you might be running away from embarrassing parents—the next, killer bees. And the ground rumbling underneath you? Could be an earthquake...could be that ginormous bully who lives next door.

Luckily, we're here to help. We've got all you need to know on how to survive just about anything. From mean teachers to lion attacks, getting dumped by a friend or surviving volcanic eruptions—we've got you covered.

You got problems? Who doesn't? Life definitely can be a scary place. But now you've got solutions.

AND, HEY, AT LEAST YOU'RE NOT BEING ATTACKED BY GRIZZLY BEARS.

HOW TO SURVIVE NATURAL DISASTERS

CHAPTER 1
A Volcanic Eruption 10

CHAPTER 2
Your Most Embarrassing
Moment 14

CHAPTER 3
A Tornado 18

CHAPTER 4
Braces 24

CHAPTER 5
Lightning 28

CHAPTER 6
A Fight 32

CHAPTER 7
An Avalanche 38

CHAPTER 8
Embarrassing Parents 42

CHAPTER 9
An Earthquake 48

CHAPTER 10
A Big Mistake 52

CHAPTER 11
A Hurricane 58

SURF'S UP!

HOW TO SURVIVE PREDATORS

CHAPTER 12
A Lion Attack 66

CHAPTER 13
Cyberbullying 70

CHAPTER 14
A Shark Attack 76

CHAPTER 15
A Mean Teacher...............................82

CHAPTER 16
A Snakebite.....................................86

CHAPTER 17
Gossip...92

CHAPTER 18
A Killer Bee Attack..........................96

CHAPTER 19
The Internet..................................102

CHAPTER 20
An Alligator or
Crocodile Attack...........................108

HOW TO SURVIVE UNCHARTERED TERRITORY

CHAPTER 21
Being the New Kid...................116

CHAPTER 22
Falling Through Ice..................122

CHAPTER 23
The Popularity Contest.............126

CHAPTER 24
A Wildfire................................132

CHAPTER 25
Throwing a Party.....................136

CHAPTER 26
A Blizzard...............................142

CHAPTER 27
A Test.....................................146

CHAPTER 28
Being Adrift at Sea..................152

CHAPTER 29
Stressing Out..........................158

CHAPTER 30
Being Lost in the Woods.........164

CHAPTER 31
A Breakup...............................170

HOW TO SURVIVE NATURAL DISASTERS

CHAPTER 1

HOW TO SURVIVE

A VOLCANIC ERUPTION

Volcanoes can be so rude. One minute they're just sitting there behaving themselves, the next they're belching and hurling all sorts of nasty stuff from their insides. And unfortunately, you can't tell a volcano to just chill. Use these survival tips when a volcano decides to blow:

BE A MAGMA MONITOR.

Just like your little sister's annoying tantrums, volcanoes give warning signs. Scientists monitor these closely, so if you're planning to hike a volcano, check with the U.S. Geological Survey to see if your mountain is about to become a monster.

THE **TALLEST** VOLCANO ON EARTH IS **MAUNA KEA IN HAWAII,** AT 30,000 FEET (9 KM) HIGH.

ROCKS 'N' ROLL.

Volcanoes are full of surprises—dangerous ones that spew out when they erupt. If you're caught in a hailstorm of red-hot rocks and can't find shelter, make like a roly-poly bug: Curl yourself into a ball and protect your head and neck.

HOLD YOUR BREATH.

Smell that fresh air! On second thought, don't! Erupting volcanoes emit poisonous carbon dioxide gases, so strap on your breathing mask while you look for shelter. Once you get inside, seal up all the doors and windows tight. Head for the highest floor possible, or at least stand on some furniture. CO_2 tends to collect near the ground, so find another place besides the floor for your volcano sleepover.

SURF'S UP!

SURF'S UP!

That wave of lava headed your way is not going to be fun to surf on. Lava can travel at 100 to 200 miles (161 to 322 km) an hour and can reach temperatures of 2,200°F (1,204°C). Unless you want to be toast (make that burnt toast!), get out of its way—fast. A ditch or creek in between you and the lava can help divert the flow away from you.

SHE'S GONNA BLOW!

Deep underground, temperatures are so hot that rock turns into a gooey liquid called magma. As it rises to the surface of the volcano, the gases in the magma are under less pressure so they expand. The volcano erupts violently when those gases escape. Now that it's out of the Earth, it's called lava.

HERE'S MUD IN YOUR EYE.

Then again, you may have bigger problems than superhot lava. Eruptions can trigger lahars—fast-flowing mixtures of melted snow, volcanic ash, and soil that will feel like a brick wall when it hits you. If it doesn't boil you alive, it might make you look like a cartoon character that's been flattened by a steamroller. Better get out of its way!

KNOW WHEN
IT BLOWS

Volcanoes are unpredictable and can erupt anytime. But here are some warning signs that might help you figure out when one is about to upchuck.

◉ Intense earthquakes may occur.

◉ The volcano acts like your grandpa and releases a lot of gas.

◉ The volcano shoots out a whole lot of steam, sort of like your dad does after you forget to take out the trash.

◉ The ground looks a little weird (like as if the surface is swollen).

SUPERVOLCANO!

Something's lurking underneath Yellowstone National Park. It has the power to kill thousands of people, destroy wildlife habitat for thousands of miles around, and plunge the Earth into a climate-changing volcanic winter for years.

It's a supervolcano. And scientists have no idea when it might explode.

Yellowstone sits on a crater (also called a caldera) that is about 28 miles (45 km) wide and 47 miles (76 km) long. It's hidden by solidified lava, forests, and even a lake, but less than ten miles below the surface, superhot magma is just waiting to explode like a shaken soda can.

The supervolcano last erupted 640,000 years ago. Scientists think that ash launched 100,000 feet (30.4 km) into the air while a thick, 1,470°F (799°C) cloud of gas, rocks, and ash swept across the land.

Could it erupt again? Absolutely—but scientists think a catastrophic eruption is highly unlikely. At least for a few thousand years.

Hopefully by then your great-great-great-times-30-grand-children will have figured out how to tame those volcanoes. Or maybe they'll be living on the moon.

CHAPTER 2

HOW TO SURVIVE

YOUR MOST EMBARRASSING MOMENT

You're making your way through the cafeteria with your tray of spaghetti and french fries. (Hey, it's a real lunch!) All of a sudden you trip, fall flat in your meatballs, get sauce all over your shirt, rip your pants, and fart. And to top it all off, your parents snap a picture because you are just…that…cute.

OK, so all these Most Embarrassing Moments (MEMs) aren't gonna happen all at once. But rest assured, you will have an MEM—everybody does! The key is how you deal with it.

LAUGH IT OFF.

Do this if you do nothing else. Show everyone that you think accidental burps are funny (because, c'mon…you know they are!). If you don't think it's a big deal, why should anyone else? Plus who's going to tease you later if they know you already think it's funny?

DON'T FREAK OUT.

Yeah, people may be laughing so hard their chocolate milk is spraying out their noses. But they're laughing at the situation. (Admit it—you would, too!) They're not laughing at you—yet. Running away or crying will only make your MEM more memorable. People will forget about your MEM, but they'll remember how you reacted.

GET SOME PERSPECTIVE.

Did your unzipped fly make you fail a test? Are your friends not speaking to you now? Is anyone in the hospital? Doubtful. Your MEM was embarrassing, but realize that there are way more important things in life to focus on.

MOVE ON.

You may think that bringing up the big ink stain on the seat of your pants over and over will show your friends that it's no big deal. Wrong. They'll get tired of hearing about your MEM, and worse, tired of assuring you it's no big thing. Forget about it, and they will, too.

PREPARE YOURSELF.

Mean kids happen, and sometimes they won't let MEMs go. Anticipate a bully's lame attempt at an insult, and have a response ready that shows you have a sense of humor about the whole thing.

COMEBACKS TO THE BIGGEST MEMS OF ALL TIME

MEM:
ACCIDENTALLY BURPING—loudly—right in the middle of your oral report on the Civil War

▶ **COMEBACK:** "I just wanted to appreciate that great lunch we had today one more time."

MEM: DROPPING YOUR TRAY IN THE CAFETERIA

▶ **COMEBACK:** "Thank you! My next performance is after gym class." (Extra points if you take a few bows.)

MEM: A STAIN ON YOUR CLOTHES

▶ **COMEBACK:** "I gave my personal butler the day off."

MEM: FALLING DOWN OR TRIPPING IN FRONT OF A CROWD

▶ **COMEBACK:** "Those ballet lessons are really paying off."

MEM: A FART IN THE MIDDLE OF CLASS

▶ **COMEBACK:** "Wow, the acoustics in here are really great."

MEM: UNZIPPED FLY

▶ **COMEBACK:** "I knew I forgot something...I just thought it was my science book."

17

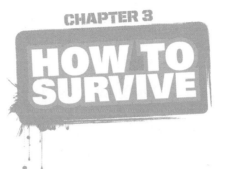

CHAPTER 3

HOW TO SURVIVE

A TORNADO

We hate to disappoint you, but a tornado is not going to pick up your house and blow you to a magical place filled with talking lions and weird little tour guides. A tornado is more likely going to bust your house apart and play keep-away with flying refrigerators. You do not want to get in a tornado's way. Here's how to stay out of it:

DON'T PANIC—YET.

A tornado watch means weather conditions might produce a tornado. A tornado warning means a twister has been spotted and may be headed for your area. Once you hear the warning—on TV, the radio, or from an emergency siren—it's time to take action.

HOW TO SURVIVE ANYTHING

MAKE LIKE A GOPHER.

The only place a tornado is guaranteed not to find you is underground, so hightail it to a basement, cellar, or storm shelter. Do not—we repeat—do not show your face skyside again until you get the all-clear from authorities.

DON'T WINDOW-SHOP.

If you don't have a basement, march your butt to a windowless, central room on the lowest floor of your house. Cramming the entire fam into a closet, bathroom, or hallway may be more quality time than you want, but it's better than watching your little sister suddenly become Supergirl.

ASSUME THE POSITION.

Crouch as low as possible to the floor and protect your head and neck with your hands and arms. Cover yourself with thick blankets or sleeping bags, and if there's a sturdy piece of furniture, like a table, crawl under it. (A bathtub offers a little protection, too.) Make sure that there's nothing like a piano directly above you on the next floor. A bookshelf crashing on top of you will not feel good either.

DRIVE. FAST.

Tornadoes treat cars like volleyballs, so you do *not* want to be stuck inside one. If you're caught in a car and the twister seems far away, watch it for a few seconds to determine its path. Compare it to a fixed object like a tree or a pole: If it's moving to the left or right, it's not moving toward you, so tell the driver to keep heading in the opposite direction of the tornado. If it appears to stay in the same place or is getting bigger, it's headed right for you. Get out of the car and seek shelter. Now.

GET OUT THE SYRUP.

If you're outside and can't find shelter, your best option is to flatten yourself on the ground like a pancake. If you see a ditch or gulley, dive in. At the very least, stay away from trees and cars, and protect your head. Do not seek shelter under bridges or overpasses. You're not a troll. Plus a tornado crashing into a bridge only leads to annihilated bridge parts flying at you.

RIDING OUT THE STORM

Most tornadoes are over in less than ten minutes, but warnings may go on for hours. Create a Tornado Time Killer to keep in your shelter. Stuff it with puzzles, books, tic-tac-toe and bingo cards, paper, and stuff to mark up the paper with. Or, pass the time in a shelter with these stupid—uh, brilliant—ideas.

◎ Give everyone—including the guys—a makeover.

◎ Have a burping contest.

◎ See who can stand on their head the longest.

◎ Draw pictures of you battling the tornado on the wall.

◎ Make up nicknames for your favorite teachers.

◎ Say the alphabet backward.

Like snowflakes, no two tornadoes are exactly alike.

There are about 1,000 tornadoes a year in the United States, far more than any other country.

Twisters can happen anywhere, but "Tornado Alley"—the name given to the states between Texas and South Dakota—gets it the worse.

Outside of the United States, Argentina and Bangladesh record the most tornadoes annually.

MYTH BUSTED!

Back in olden times, people were told to crack their windows during a tornado to equalize the pressure so their houses wouldn't explode. Turns out the twister is going to tear apart your house long before anything like that happens. Today, smart survivors stay away from windows altogether.

CHAPTER 4

HOW TO SURVIVE

BRACES

Not looking forward to having a mouthful of metal for the next two years? We don't blame you. But unless you want to look like Austin Powers, you gotta wear 'em. Here's how to make your ordeal a little less painful:

PIG OUT.

The day before you go get your braces, eat everything that will be on the no-no list once you're covered in metal: Tootsie Rolls, apples, caramel, nuts, popcorn, hard candy, whatever! It'll be the one time your mom won't complain too much about you spoiling your dinner.

PLAY UP THE SYMPATHY CARD.

After you get braces or have them tightened, your teeth will be a little too sore to eat solid food for a day or two. Make people feel sorry for you so you can take advantage of the situation and live off milkshakes, smoothies, and cheesy soup.

ACCESSORIZE.

Have fun with those little rubber bands your orthodontist gives you. Try out different hues to match your outfit or your school colors. Go for a theme, like orange and black for Halloween or green for St. Patrick's Day.

SMILE.

Trying to hide your braces by never opening your mouth is not gonna fly. People will just wonder what's up, so act like you normally do and give your best friend's joke the belly laugh it deserves.

FUH-GED-UH-BOWD-IT.

You know how sometimes you can't remember if a friend wears glasses, or if your dad has a mustache? Pretty soon your braces are just going to be part of who you are. Chances are, people aren't even going to notice them after a while.

DON'T STORE DESSERT IN YOUR TEETH.

Bits of food in your braces is just gross and gives you bad breath (not to mention cavities). It's a pain, but try to brush and floss after every meal.

WHAT'S THE POINT?

So, here's the deal: Your adult teeth grow in as your baby teeth fall out. Sometimes adult teeth don't come in straight. The good news is that this is one thing you really can blame your parents for. Crooked or overlapping teeth and mismatched jawlines that cause under- or overbites are often hereditary. The bad news is that if you've inherited not-so-perfect teeth, you probably have to get braces.

The concept behind braces is pretty simple. They stay in place for a long time (usually six months to two years) and keep steady pressure on your teeth. That's what all those annoying wires, springs, and rubber bands are for—to create tension against your teeth. Eventually the constant pressure of the braces will change the arrangement of your teeth.

Can you live without braces? Sure. But crooked teeth affect how you chew, so it might be hard for you to enjoy pizza night or fried chicken at a picnic. They also make it hard to brush, which can lead to tooth decay and cavities. So which would you rather be: the kid with braces for a couple years, or the kid with missing teeth who can't eat a crunchy chocolate bar—ever?

CHECKLIST FOR THE DAY YOU GET YOUR BRACES

Lip balm (unless you want cracked lips after having your mouth propped open for two hours)

iPod or book to pass the time

Unlimited supply of milkshakes and frozen yogurt waiting at home

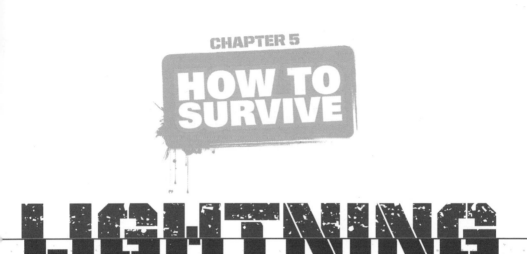

CHAPTER 5

HOW TO SURVIVE

LIGHTNING

Maybe this wasn't the best idea you've ever had. You figured you had plenty of time to walk home before the storm. Wrong. Now the lightning is so close you're wondering if you're going to be sporting the troll doll look soon. Avoid becoming a human Glow Stick with these easy tips:

▶ SEEK SHELTER.

If you see lightning and can't count to 30 before you hear thunder, get into an enclosed structure or vehicle as soon as you can. If you're in a house, close all the windows, and don't take baths or showers or wash dishes. Avoid using anything that will put you in contact with electricity (such as TVs and landlines—that phone call to Grandma will just have to wait), and stay away from anything metal. Remain inside for 30 minutes after the last thunderclap.

IF YOU CAN HEAR THUNDER, YOU'RE IN STRIKING RANGE OF LIGHTNING.

DON'T BE A TREE HUGGER.

Lightning often strikes the tallest thing around, so don't look for shelter under tall trees. That goes double for telephone or electrical poles, unless you want to be the next flash in a fireworks display.

GO SWIMMING LATER.

Water is conductive, meaning it can transfer the lightning's electricity to you. Stay away from bodies of water, even puddles. If you're in the pool, get out!

LIGHTEN THE LOAD.

Metal is also conductive. If you're wearing anything with metal in it—a backpack, a belt, jewelry—now's the time to get rid of it. Who'da thought your mom would welcome a lightning storm, but it means you will finally take those headphones out of your ears!

SHORTEN IT UP.

If you're out in the open, make yourself as small as possible. Crouch with your head between your knees. Don't lie flat. The ground is conductive, so you want as little of your body touching it as possible.

BECOME A LONER.

When is a group hug not a good idea? When that group hug is like sitting in the electric chair. If you're with a bunch of people, space yourselves about 15 feet (4.5 m) apart so the lightning won't jump from person to person.

LIGHTNING BOLT
ATTRACTION

LIGHTNING IS FIVE TIMES HOTTER THAN THE SURFACE OF THE SUN.

Scientists aren't sure exactly how lightning forms. One theory is sort of like an old-school love story. Within the cloud, smaller particles become positively charged. Let's call them Juliets. Larger particles become negatively charged. We'll call them Romeos. These particles become separated, with the Juliets at the top of the cloud and the Romeos at the bottom. But nothing—not even the air's resistance to electrical flow—can keep these lovers apart. Their attraction—or electrical potential—is too strong, so the Romeos and Juliets charge into each other's metaphorical arms, completing an electrical circuit. The result is electric. Literally. All that pent-up electricity is released, which causes lightning.

THUNDER SECRETS REVEALED!
The intense heat from lightning causes the surrounding air to expand rapidly. When it does, it creates thunder.

MYTH BUSTED!
Touching someone who's been struck by lightning will not shock you. Get that person to a hospital as soon as is safely possible.

IMPRESS YOUR FRIENDS!
Count the seconds between the lightning flash and the thunder, then divide by five. That's how many miles away the lightning is.

31

CHAPTER 6

HOW TO SURVIVE

A FIGHT

You thought you were just kidding around when you teased your best friend about not getting to class on time, but now all of a sudden you're screaming at each other in the hallway. Or maybe you and a friend were arguing over who screwed up the play at the basketball tournament, and you ended up in a shoving match.

When a fight between friends happens, it's not really important who started it, or who's right and who's wrong. To keep your friendship strong, you have to make up and move on.

DUELING IS STILL LEGAL IN PARAGUAY, HOWEVER, BOTH PARTIES MUST BE REGISTERED BLOOD DONORS.

COOL OFF.

Step away from the situation and take a few deep breaths—or maybe a million. When you're angry or upset, you're more likely to say things you can't take back and will regret later. (Things like "You eat like a cow" or "You're too dumb to understand *Dumb and Dumber*" come to mind.) Give yourself and your friend some space to chill out.

DO A PRIVATE PLAY-BY-PLAY.

Remind yourself about all aspects of the fight. Where did it happen? Who was involved? What led up to it? Be honest when asking yourself why you were fighting ("Because he's a jerk" is not an answer), and what you're really angry about. If a fight started after you made fun of a friend's 32nd retelling of her star performance as Nun Number Two in *The Sound of Music*, figure out if it's really because you think she's always trying to upstage your stories—or if you might be a little bit jealous of her success.

SHUT YOUR MOUTH.

Do not start bad-mouthing a friend or posting embarrassing pictures on Facebook. If you want to stay friends, this is not the way to do it.

GET SOME FACE TIME.

Clapping when a friend has dropped a tray in the cafeteria isn't just going to go away. When you've both calmed down, ask your friend if you can talk about what happened—even if you don't think the fight was your fault. Pick a place away from other people who might offer up opinions and make things worse. Just don't wait too long: Bad feelings will build up and make it that much harder to get over it.

TAKE A LITTLE RESPONSIBILITY.

First, apologize for your role in the fight. (C'mon, you know you're not blameless.) A simple "I'm sorry I overreacted" or "I'm sorry I called you horseface" can ease your way into the conversation and make it easier for your friend to apologize, too.

TALK IT OUT.

Explain why you felt hurt or got angry, and let your friend do the same. Listen to what each other has to say. Don't offer up excuses ("I wouldn't have ditched you at the mall if you hadn't been so busy texting") or get defensive ("I am not obsessed with my little sister's My Pretty Pony collection!"). Avoid "You did this" statements; they just make it seem like you're attacking your friend.

DON'T STRIKE A POSE.

Nothing says "I don't respect what you're saying" more than rolling your eyes, crossing your arms across your chest, or putting your hands on your hips.

ANY SOLUTION IS BETTER THAN NO SOLUTION.

A conversation ending with one person saying "I'm so sorry, it was all my fault, I'll never do that again" is probably not going to happen. It's more likely that both of you need to make concessions, with one person saying, "I know baseball is important to you, so I understand that you have to spend a lot of time at practice," and the other saying, "Yes, but I'll try not to take baseball so seriously."

HUG IT OUT.

You've smoothed things over with your friend. Now don't screw it up! Move beyond the fight. Don't hold a grudge or bring it up later.

HOW TO SAY "I'M SORRY"

We all screw up. Whether you've ignored your friend in the cafeteria or punched someone in anger, sometimes you have to swallow your pride and apologize. Here's how.

◉ Understand what you're apologizing for. Clearly state what you've done wrong.

◉ Do not offer excuses or blame anyone else for their role in your screw-up.

◉ No "ifs" or "buts." That puts the blame back on the person you're apologizing to.

◉ Look the person in the eye. Avoid any 'tude on your part by keeping your hands at your side or on a table in front of you.

◉ Be prepared for knee-jerk responses like, "You *should* be sorry!" Let your friend vent for a second, then keep going.

◉ Offer a solution, and promise it won't happen again. (Then don't let it happen again!)

◉ Give your friend time to forgive you.

◉ Move on. Do not keep apologizing or asking if your friend is still mad.

SAY THIS, NOT THAT

SAY THIS
"I'm sorry I lost your sunglasses."

> **NOT THAT**
"I'm sorry I lost your sunglasses, but my mom was screaming at me that I was going to be late for school."

SAY THIS
"I'm sorry I asked your crush to study after school."

> **NOT THAT**
"I'm sorry I asked your crush to study, but you act like you don't like him anymore."

SAY THIS
"I'm sorry I said you throw like my grandma."

> **NOT THAT**
"I'm sorry if you got upset when I said you throw like my grandma."

SAY THIS
"It was wrong of me to call you 'jigglebutt.'"

> **NOT THAT**
"I'm sorry I called you 'jigglebutt' but you really do eat a lot."

SAY THIS
"I'm sorry I pulled your chair out from under you."

> **NOT THAT**
"I'm sorry I pulled out your chair from under you, but you know I like to pull pranks."

CHAPTER 7

HOW TO SURVIVE

AN AVALANCHE

Ever wonder what it would feel like to be tossed around in a giant washing machine filled with chunks of snow? That's pretty much what getting caught in an avalanche feels like. And when the raging rapids of snow actually stop, you'll be stuck like a bug in a vanilla milkshake. Here are a few tips to prevent future generations from having to thaw you out like a woolly mammoth.

USE YOUR OUTSIDE VOICE.

If you see an avalanche coming, shout to let your friends know you're about to become a human snowball. That way, they can keep an eye on you and hopefully figure out where you end up. If you're skiing, toss your poles and try to step out of your skis. They'll just pull you deeper into the snow.

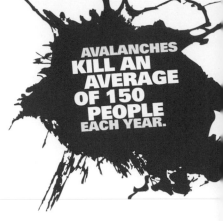

AVALANCHES KILL AN AVERAGE OF 150 PEOPLE EACH YEAR.

GO FOR THE GOLD.

A human body in moving snow is like the *Titanic*: It sinks. To stay on top of the avalanche, move your arms like you're swimming for the most important Olympic medal ever.

DON'T GOSSIP.

Keep your mouth shut so snow doesn't pack into your throat. Oh wait, you want to breathe? Do it through your nose.

GIVE YOURSELF SOME SPACE.

As the avalanche slows, curve your arms in front of your face and chest to create an air pocket. Then shove one arm above the surface so people can find you. Stay calm—you're gonna need all the oxygen you can get, and struggling uses it up.

ROCK ON.

Compacted snow is like a recording studio: soundproof. Don't waste oxygen by shouting for help until you hear rescuers close by. Then scream like a rock star.

MYTH BUSTED!

Loud noises do not cause avalanches, unless they're extremely loud, like an explosive going off nearby. (If that happens, then you have way bigger problems than an avalanche to worry about!)

AN AVALANCHE CAN TRAVEL UP TO 80 MILES (129 KM) AN HOUR.

HOW IT WORKS

There are several types of avalanches, but the deadliest is called a slab avalanche. This occurs when a soft or weak layer of snow is covered by a harder layer. The weak layer can't support the packed layer on top of it, so when a skier, snowboarder, or hiker puts extra weight on the snow, the weaker layer collapses, fracturing the top layer and causing an avalanche.

HOW TO SPOT AN AVALANCHE

Almost all fatal avalanches occur in the backcountry, away from ski areas. Never go into avalanche zones alone, and keep your group spread out. (Who's going to rescue you if everyone's buried?) And watch for these warning signs.

Extremely windy conditions

Steep terrain

New snow

Recent rain

Broken trees

Quickly rising temperatures

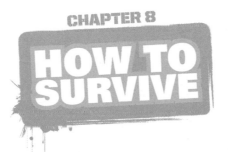

CHAPTER 8

HOW TO SURVIVE

EMBARRASSING PARENTS

Your dad singing Sinatra tunes at the top of his lungs in the elevator. Your mom wearing her holiday sweater—complete with jingle bells and blinking red Rudolph nose—till past New Year's. Your parents continuing to call you Poopy Monster   your nickname after one tiny accident you had when you were two—in front of your friends.

Roll your eyes all you want, but your parents will always find ways to embarrass you. Not that they mean to—they probably have no clue that their fondness for all-you-can-eat buffets makes you cringe. Luckily, there are ways to deal with embarrassing parents.

PUT YOURSELF IN THEIR SOCKS-AND-SANDALS.

Think about why your parents behave like they do. Your mom may be wearing clothes from the Clinton administration because she's saving money to buy you new things. That story your dad tells—over and over—about the time you cut your own bangs may be embarrassing to you, but to him it's a reminder of how happy you've made him. Understanding their behavior might make it a little more tolerable.

ACCORDING TO A UK SURVEY BY YOUNGPOLL.COM, 7 OUT OF 10 KIDS AGES 6 TO 15 REPORT FEELING "HUMILIATED" BY THEIR PARENTS AT SOME POINT OR ANOTHER.

MAKE A TOP TEN LIST.

Write down what embarrasses you about your parents. Then prioritize: Which ones drive you the craziest? Which ones can you actually change? You may be able to stop your mom from calling your friends "dude," but getting your dad to trade in his beat-up, canary-yellow truck for a Jag probably isn't going to happen.

HAVE AN INTERVENTION.

Talk to your parents about what's bugging you. Even if they were good-naturedly trying to embarrass you a little, they probably don't realize how much it hurts you. See the tips at the end of the chapter on how to bring up embarrassing behavior—without embarrassing yourself.

CREATE A CODE.

Even if your parents agree to stop their embarrassing behavior, they'll probably slip from time to time. (After all, they've been wiping smudges off your cheek with their spit since your very first encounter with spaghetti sauce.) Establish a signal that says, "Mom, you're doing it again," without embarrassing anyone.

DON'T BE A SCENE STEALER.

Avoid the urge to cry out, "DAD!" or storm from a room when your parents are embarrassing you. That only draws attention to the situation and makes things worse. Ignore the behavior, take some breaths, and deal with things when you're more calm.

REMEMBER: YOUR FRIENDS HAVE PARENTS, TOO.

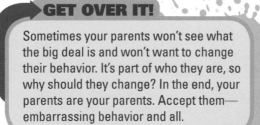

Your friends will not 1. assume you talk back to the television just because your mom does, 2. think less of you because your dad dresses your German shepherd in a pink tutu, or 3. refuse to come to school dances because your parents boogie while they're chaperoning. The truth is, your friends' parental units are just as embarrassing; they probably barely notice how goofy your parents can be.

GET OVER IT!

Sometimes your parents won't see what the big deal is and won't want to change their behavior. It's part of who they are, so why should they change? In the end, your parents are your parents. Accept them—embarrassing behavior and all.

KNOW THE DIFFERENCE

If a parent's behavior is more dangerous than embarrassing—drinking too much, starting fights, demeaning you in public—talk to a trusted adult, such as a coach, a teacher, or an older sibling.

BLUSHING SECRETS REVEALED!

When you're embarrassed, your body releases adrenaline. It's the same chemical that's released when you're scared or in danger. Among other things, adrenaline causes your blood vessels to dilate, or expand, so that more oxygen-rich blood can flow through your body. This is great if you need an energy boost to escape from a hungry bear. But if you're just standing around being embarrassed after your parents sucked helium out of party balloons and started singing like Alvin and the Chipmunks, all that blood flow to your cheeks just makes you look red.

PARENTAL TALKING TIPS

Speak calmly; don't shout.

Listen to what they have to say.

Don't insult your parents personally; address their behavior instead. For instance, "Sometimes your 'woo-hooing' when I'm up to bat makes me uncomfortable" is much better than, "You sound like an idiot when you 'woo-hoo.'"

Be prepared to explain why the behavior embarrasses you.

Offer a solution, not a demand or ultimatum. For instance, "I know you like to talk to strangers in the grocery store line, but maybe you could just do it when I'm not there" is easier to take than, "If you keep talking to strangers in line I will never go anywhere with you again."

CHAPTER 9

HOW TO SURVIVE

AN EARTHQUAKE

The good news: During an earthquake, the ground is 99.9999999 percent not likely to open up and swallow you whole. The bad news: All the flying debris and falling buildings could do you in—and if not, the fires and tsunamis that the earthquake triggers just might.

If you remember one thing (and in an earthquake, you'll be lucky to remember your name), it's this: Drop, cover, and hold on. Here's what we mean.

MAKE A TABLE YOUR NEW BFF.

An earthquake and its aftershocks can last a few seconds or a couple minutes, and sometimes there's no time to get to the absolute safest place in the building. Get underneath something sturdy, like a doorframe or a table, and hold on.

TAKE A RIDE.

If whatever you're under starts to slide, hang on and slide with it. Kind of like a Slip 'n' Slide—only scarier.

STAND IN THE CORNER.

The next best place is inside a corner of a building. Make sure you're as far away from windows as possible. Watching nature's biggest rock 'n' roll concert might be kinda cool, but even a punk rocker doesn't want a faceful of glass.

SLEEP IN.

An earthquake jerking you out of a dream involving you, a pile of money, and 18 monkeys dressed like butlers is no way to wake up. Still, stay in bed facedown with a pillow over your head and neck with one hand, and with the other hold on to the mattress like it's about to become a flying carpet.

DON'T GET DISTRACTED.

Burglar alarms may be screaming in your ear, and you might be taking an early shower when the sprinkler system is triggered by all the shaking. Stay calm and remain right where you are. Do not try to change locations once you've found your safe spot.

A 9.2 MAGNITUDE EARTHQUAKE— THE LARGEST EVER RECORDED— SHOOK CHILE IN 1960.

PLAN FOR THE GREAT OUTDOORS.

If you're outside, try to head to an open space away from buildings or power lines. If you're in the mountains, watch out for falling rocks and landslides. Earthquake interrupt your beach vacation? Head to higher ground.

EARTHQUAKE ADVICE

During a temblor, stay far, far away from these things. (OK, some of them are just for fun!)

- ⊚ Windows
- ⊚ Light fixtures and ceiling fans
- ⊚ Wall hangings and bookshelves
- ⊚ Outside doors and walls
- ⊚ Elevators
- ⊚ Streetlights, power lines, and trees
- ⊚ Rooms full of soda bottles
- ⊚ Bowls of hot soup

HIGH MAGNITUDE

A 6.3-magnitude earthquake. A 7.6-magnitude temblor. Earthquakes are often described with these obscure numbers, even though few people know what they actually mean. Here's the scoop: The magnitude is simply one way scientists measure the size of earthquakes. All the vibrations created by the earthquake create waves of energy. (It's kind of like how tossing a rock into a lake will cause little waves to ripple out from the rock.) It's these seismic waves that scientists are measuring when they talk about magnitude. The bigger the vibrations, the bigger the wave, and the stronger the earthquake. (Each whole number on the Richter scale is ten times stronger than the previous one.) For the most part, you can't feel an earthquake with a magnitude of 2.0 or less. Damage usually doesn't occur until an earthquake hits a 4 or 5 magnitude.

CHAPTER 10

HOW TO SURVIVE

A BIG MISTAKE

It's the night of the school talent show, and the spotlight's on you. You've been working for weeks perfecting your saxophone solo, and now it's time for you to show the audience your awesomeness. You take a deep breath, blow, and... hear something come out of the sax that sounds like you've been eating chili nonstop for a week!

Whether you've blown a line in a school play or scored a goal for the other team, big mistakes can be mortifying. You feel like you've let your friends down and that everyone's thinking, "What a jerk." But don't let a simple mistake turn into the blunder of the century. Minimize the damage with these helpful hints.

IN 1943, JAMES WRIGHT WAS TRYING TO MAKE A SUBSTITUTE FOR RUBBER WHEN HE ACCIDENTALLY INVENTED SILLY PUTTY.

MAKE SURE THE SHOW GOES ON.

We're not sure how you could forget the line, "To be or not to be, that is the question." But, hey, stuff happens. Stay in character, start with a line you do remember, and keep going. If you're on the field, keep the action moving, shake it off, and get ready for the next play. By making your mistake a blip instead of a blunder, everyone can move on and forget it ever happened. (Bonus: They'll be impressed with your quick thinking. Now you're awesome again.)

OWN IT.

No one wants to hear, "If you hadn't been so slow I wouldn't have blown the handoff in the relay." That just makes you look like a whiner. Don't point fingers or try to explain away what happened (even if you think you have reason to). Just admit you made a mistake and keep it all on you; people will respect that you took responsibility.

BE A COMEDIAN.

A mistake can be embarrassing, but don't turn one into your Most Embarrassing Moment. Remember, everyone makes mistakes, and people tend to forgive them—as long as you forgive them, too! Start with a preemptive strike and be the first to acknowledge the mistake. "I guess my update of Shakespeare didn't go over so well." "I thought I was performing for a bunch of kindergartners who wouldn't know the difference between Mozart and what I came up with." "Sorry—I got our playbook and the other team's playbook confused."

> ### SHRUG IT OFF.
> Crying, freezing up, or running away like a wimpy kid only brings more attention to your mistake. If you act like it's a big deal, so will others.

> ### THINK ON IT.
> Now that everyone's moved on, take a closer look at what happened. Was this a onetime mistake or something that's happened before? What really went wrong—were you being careless? Did you not know how to do what you were supposed to do? Did something distract you? Were you truly prepared? Figuring out why the mistake happened—then taking action—will help make sure it doesn't happen again.

NO BIGGIE

It's normal to freak a little before participating in a big event, whether it's an important game, a school musical, or just a presentation in class. And it's not just mental. Your heart beating like an out-of-control drumroll is your body's reaction to fear: Stress hormones like adrenaline are released into the bloodstream, which causes—among other things—your heart to pump more oxygen-rich blood to your brain and muscles to help you stay focused, strong, and alert. It's a survival response commonly called fight-or-flight. Our ancestors used it to swim away from crocodiles or spear lions. You use it to survive your piano solo. (Same thing, right?)

But too much nervousness can lead to mistakes. Remember these chill-out tips to breathe easy before a big performance.

Drive Your Family Crazy. The more you practice, the better you're going to know your stuff (even if your parents are sick of listening to your monologue for the millionth time). So if you're preparing for a big concert, rehearse an extra 15 minutes a day. If you're about to give

your election-day speech for the Student Council, read it over and over in front of friends or family. Focus on areas that are giving you trouble. If you keep flubbing a line in rehearsal, repeat it 20 times—until it's impossible to screw up.

Pump Yourself Up. Building up your confidence is a great way to calm those butterflies. Look in the mirror and repeat, "You're gonna do great!" (Just make sure no one is listening, unless you never want to hear the end of it.) Gather teammates before a game to sing the school song or do a crazy chant. (Bonus: That may make the other team nervous!) Leave yourself little notes about how awesome you are. Your little sister may not agree, but what does she know?

Just Relax. Take some deep breaths. Listen to music. Go for a walk. Whatever your favorite chill-out method is, relaxing will take your mind off your big event and help calm you down.

Reward Yourself. Tell yourself that once you ace that 15-minute oral report, you're allowed to do something fun like splurge on that video game you've been eyeing. You'll have something to look forward to, and it's cool to congratulate yourself for how great you are.

I SURVIVED A MISTAKE

The whole world saw these mistakes, and yet these folks survived. If famous people can shrug off mistakes and move on, so can you.

Singer and actress Jennifer Lopez fell on her butt during a dance routine at the televised 2009 American Music Awards. Lopez popped back up and seamlessly transitioned into a solo dance performance.

Early in the 2008 season of *American Idol*, contestant David Archuleta forgot the lyrics to the song he was performing on national TV. The 17-year-old managed to recover and was voted first-runner-up for the show and snagged a major recording contract.

In 1948, the *Chicago Daily Tribune*, along with other newspapers, mistakenly printed the headline "Dewey Defeats Truman" after polls incorrectly predicted Thomas Dewey would beat Harry S. Truman in the presidential election. (Truman became the 33rd President of the United States.) Despite the blunder, the *Tribune* is still in business, though today it's just called the *Chicago Tribune*.

In 1992, then-Vice President Dan Quayle "corrected" a student at a spelling bee, telling him that the word "potato" should be spelled "potatoe." Despite the mistake, Quayle went on to become a best-selling author and successful businessman after he left politics.

Indianapolis Colts quarterback Peyton Manning threw an interception that was returned by the other team for a touchdown during the 2010 Super Bowl. The Colts lost to the New Orleans Saints, but Manning is still considered one of the greatest quarterbacks ever.

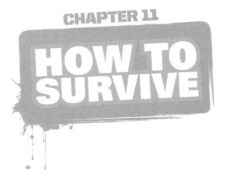

CHAPTER 11

HOW TO SURVIVE

A HURRICANE

f the first thing you do when a hurricane is headed your way is pull out your surfboard and hit the beach, then this chapter is not for you. If you actually want to survive, read on.

READY, SET...BLOW!

The best thing about hurricanes? Unlike tornadoes, you get a decent amount of warning before they hit. As soon as officials announce a hurricane watch for your area, start making preparations.

IN AUSTRALIA, SOME PEOPLE CALL HURRICANES WILLY-WILLIES.

GO DOOR-TO-DOOR.

Check on your neighbors who might need help. Ask your parents permission to invite them to bunker down at your house, or offer them a space in your car if you're evacuating. If they're sick or elderly, remind them to bring their medication. The more people hanging out, the more people you can beat at Pictionary.

CLEAN UP YOUR YARD.

Funny thing about hurricanes: Even if you know they're coming, you're never exactly sure where they're going to hit. Take precautions anyway. Ask your parents to gas up the car in case you need to evacuate. Bring in any lawn furniture or other stuff that can blow away—or through a window—and anchor down what can't be moved. Board up your windows or crisscross them with heavy strips of tape to keep glass from shattering.

HOMEBODY RULES

If your family decides to stay put instead of evacuate, make sure to follow these rules:

◎ Fill all bathtubs and sinks with clean, cold water in case the water lines are damaged or the supply becomes contaminated.

◎ Set the refrigerator to maximum cool and keep the door closed. This will help keep your food from becoming furry if there's a power outage.

◎ Ride out the storm in an interior room, such as a closet or hallway. Don't even think about going near a window, even if it's boarded up.

◎ Close all interior doors to protect yourself from flying glass.

◎ Stay inside. A sudden calm probably means that the eye of the storm—the center of the hurricane—is passing over you. More hurricane fun is on its way.

BE A HERO
STASH A SURVIVAL KIT

A hurricane may last all day, but the aftermath—power outages, water shortages, limited rescue teams—can last a while. If you're riding out the storm, make sure you've got an emergency kit stocked with the following:

Water: about one gallon per person per day for at least three days

Food: enough non-perishable items, such as canned goods and dry cereal, for at least three days (Don't forget the can opener)

Battery-powered or hand-cranked radio, plus extra batteries

Wrench or pliers to turn off utilities

Flashlight and extra batteries

First-aid kit

Moist towelettes and garbage bags for when you gotta, uh, go

Whistle

Food and water for your pet

Prescription meds and glasses

Dust mask, plastic sheeting, duct tape

Matches

A hurricane forms when warm air rising from the ocean collides with cooler winds higher up. Water temperature must be at least 80 degrees Fahrenheit (26.7 degrees Celsius).

The deadliest hurricane of all time hit East Pakistan (now Bangla-desh) in 1970 and caused an estimated 300,000 deaths.

Hurricanes weaken when they hit land because their power source—warm ocean water—is gone.

A tropical storm becomes a Category One hurricane when winds reach 74 miles (119 km) an hour. The worst hurricanes—Category Fives—have winds at more than 155 miles (249 km) an hour.

Cyclical tropical storms like hurricanes are also called "cyclones" or "typhoons."

The strongest part of the hurricane is right before and after the calm center of the storm, called the eye. A typical eye is about 20 miles (32 km) across.

HOW TO SURVIVE
PREDATORS

RIGHT

WRONG

CHAPTER 12

HOW TO SURVIVE

A LION ATTACK

Pop Quiz: What's the difference between an African lion and a mountain lion? If you guessed that one lives in Africa— you're right! (Not to mention the fact that it's four times bigger than the other.) But when it comes to surviving an attack from either of these predators, your strategy to keep from becoming lunch meat is just about the same.

MOUNTAIN LIONS ARE ALSO CALLED PUMAS, COUGARS, CATAMOUNTS, AND PANTHERS.

BE A PEOPLE PERSON.

Lions—both African and mountain—usually avoid humans. If you're hiking in their territory, bring your friends and use your outside voices. Shake your keys. Sing those songs your parents hate. Loudly. It'll be just like a zoo—only the lion will be the one observing from a distance and snickering at your behavior.

MAKE LIKE A STATUE.

You know how a pet cat gets a kick out of chasing a mouse? In this case, you're the mouse. It might be your first instinct, but don't turn your back on a lion and run—it'll only see a hot meal on legs and chase you. Instead, freeze…then calmly back away.

BRING OUT YOUR BULLY SIDE.

Big cats prefer an easy kill, so if it's still coming at you as you're quietly trying to walk away, make it think you're king of the jungle…or forest. Don't crouch, kneel, or play dead. Instead, scream, snarl, and bare your teeth. Raise your arms or open your jacket to appear bigger.

GO TEN ROUNDS.

If the cat's still coming at you, fight back. Swing a big stick, hurl rocks, or even poke at its eyeballs if it gets really close.

AN AFRICAN LION'S ROAR CAN BE HEARD UP TO FIVE MILES AWAY.

AFRICAN LION

SIZE
as much as
420 pounds
(191 kg)

RANGE
sub-Saharan
Africa

DIET
antelope,
zebra, wilde-
beest

FAMILY
pride often
consists of three
males, a dozen related
females, and their
young

MOUNTAIN LION

RANGE
western United
States and Canada,
parts of Florida, parts
of Mexico and Central
and South
America

SIZE
up to 140
pounds
(64 kg)

DIET
deer and
smaller animals
such as raccoons
and coyotes

FAMILY
solitary; moms
may have a cub
or two

CHAPTER 13

HOW TO SURVIVE

CYBER-BULLYING

OMG LOL! You and your BFF got in a fight, so now her buds are posting mean messages on your Facebook page to get revenge. Yeah. (Enter sarcastic tone here.) Hil-lar-ious. About 81 percent of teens think that cyberbullies do their thing because they think it's funny, according to the National Crime Prevention Council. But if you're like nearly half of all kids, you've been affected by cyberbullying and know it's definitely not a joke. Here's how to beat the bullies at their own stupid game:

BULLY BLOCKAGE.

If someone's sending you mean emails or posting nasty things on your Facebook page, block them. More than 70 percent of teens say this is the best defense against an online bully.

ABOUT **THREE OUT OF EVERY FOUR TEENS** WHO ARE CYBERBULLIED EVENTUALLY FIND OUT WHO THEIR NEMESIS IS.

TALK TO THE CYBERHAND.

Remember when your parents told you to ignore those playground bullies giving kids atomic wedgies? Same thing goes here. Most bullies—including cyber ones—just want to get a reaction out of you, so don't give them what they want.

LEAVE THE ROOM.

U R stupid. I H8 U. Messages like these are uncool, so if you get them while you're IMing or in a chat room, just sign off.

TRASH IT.

Don't open messages from people you don't know, or from known bullies. Just delete them.

SURPRISE: **IT'S USUALLY SOMEONE** FROM SCHOOL.

BE A CSI.

A couple mean messages? Just ignore. But if you start feeling constantly harassed, it's time to collect evidence. Start saving the bully's messages, photos, and IMs.

DO THE UNTHINKABLE.

That's right. Tell an adult. They may be clueless about how to send a text message, but they can help you deal with cyberbullies.

IF ALL ELSE FAILS, CALL IN REINFORCEMENTS.

If an adult feels like it's beyond their control, they can contact your cell phone or Internet service provider. Service providers can help track down anonymous bullies, purge Web sites of offending messages, and take action against e-meanies.

I H8 U!
BLOCK

BE A STAND-UP GUY (OR GIRL)

Even if you're not the one being cyberbullied, you can still help stop it.

C'mon! If a friend is cyberbullying someone, tell him to stop.

Tell an adult—a teacher, a coach, or even a parent—that someone's being dumped on in cyberspace.

Refuse to go on to Web sites created to hurt or embarrass someone.

Don't forward mean or untrue messages.

Block communication with cyberbullies who make fun of other people.

WHAT'S CONSIDERED CYBERBULLYING?

Cyberbullying may seem like harmless fun, but it can get you in big trouble—sometimes with the police. Be smart: Use the Internet and cell phones to keep in touch with friends, but stay away from uncool behaviors like these.

Posting or emailing photos of someone without their permission

Creating a fake email account and sending mean messages pretending to be another person

Creating or participating in a Web site designed to hurt someone else

Spreading lies and rumors on the Internet

MORE THAN 40 OF THE 50 UNITED STATES MAKE BULLYING IN SOME FORM ILLEGAL.

Sending harassing or threatening emails, text messages, or IMs

Posting mean messages on social networking sites (like Facebook), blogs, or chat rooms

FACE-TO-FACE WITH A BULLY

Believe it or not, once there was no such thing as the Internet. So there was no cyberbullying. But just because bullies have found another way to harass you doesn't mean that the old-fashioned, in-your-face kind of bullying has gone the way of the black-and-white TV. Physical violence and relentless teasing still exist. Here's how to survive:

Safety in Numbers. Bullies don't want to mess with a pack. Try to always have a friend or two with you walking home, in the bathroom, on the bus, or anywhere else a bully may seek you out.

Use the Silent Treatment. Stand up straight, hold your head up high, and just walk away. A bully is usually just trying to get a reaction by making you cry or fight, so don't give the meanie the satisfaction.

Stand Strong. In a strong, confident voice, tell the bully to stop. Don't be insulting, but show that you think the behavior is uncool. "Does shoving me against a locker really make you feel that powerful?" or "What are we, 8 years old?" Now you've got the bully questioning those actions, which gives you a little more control. But try not to say anything that can be heard by a lot of people. That'll just embarrass your enemy and probably make things worse.

Start a Campaign. If your school doesn't already have one, start an anti-bullying program. Talk to your principal about asking students to sign a petition pledging to stand up to bullying. Hold an anti-bullying assembly, and invite experts to speak and give advice. Host a blog where classmates can write about their own experiences with bullies.

Help, Please! No one wants to enlist an adult's help, but sometimes there's no other choice. You can manage to be sneaky about it, though. Try calling a teacher or principal before or after school so no one sees you going into her office. Or, send an anonymous email to alert school administrators they have a bully problem.

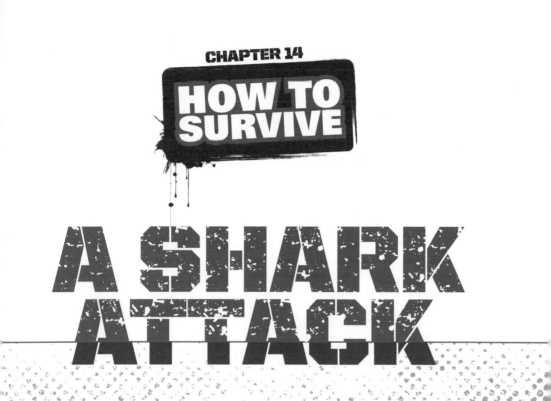

CHAPTER 14

HOW TO SURVIVE

A SHARK ATTACK

Wouldn't it be great if all sharks were vegetarians? Or if the only purpose of all those teeth was to flash a friendly smile? Nothing will get swimmers out of the ocean faster than a shark lurking in the water. Shark attacks are rare, but still, who wants to be on the menu when you're just trying to have a little fun? Here's what to do in case it looks like you're about to become shark bait.

DON'T PANIC.

You know what one of a shark's favorite snacks is? A seal. And you know what you look like when you are frantically swimming away from a shark? (Ten points if you said, "A seal.") Stay calm. Breathe. Chances are that the shark's just curious about this weird bathing-suited creature in the water and will move along in search of something more familiar.

SAY, "RIBBIT!"

You can't outswim a shark. But you *have* to try to get out of the water—fast. Dog paddling and other splashy styles will make you look as yummy as, well, a dog. So instead, use underwater motions such as the froglike breaststroke to get to dry land.

OF THE **400** **SPECIES** OF SHARK WORLDWIDE, **LESS THAN 12** ARE CONSIDERED DANGEROUS TO HUMANS.

FIGHT BACK.

Unlike human beings, a shark is not gonna listen to a strong, confident "Leave me alone!" demand. If a shark gets too close—or worse, starts treating your leg as an all-you-can-eat buffet—start swinging. Hit, punch, kick, anything to let the shark know you're not easy prey. Aim for its soft spots—like gills and eyes—and use anything hard you may have with you, such as a camera or a mask.

DON'T BACK DOWN.

Once you start fighting back, keep fighting. Sharks may be big and scary, but they're kinda lazy. If you show them you're too much trouble, they'll probably move on to easier pickings.

GET SMART

The best way to not be attacked by a shark? Avoid things that attract sharks!

Swim in groups. Sharks are much more likely to attack lone swimmers. Groups of people can also keep an eye out for circling sharks and help if someone is attacked.

Have movie night. Sharks tend to hunt from dusk to dawn, so stay out of the water when the sun goes down.

Leave the bling at home. Shiny stuff like watches, necklaces, and earrings can look like fish scales to a hungry shark.

Don't use the ocean as your own personal toilet. Sharks are attracted to strong smells, including urine. So if you gotta go, hold it till you're out of the water (and off the beach…no one wants to see that!).

Don't be like raw meat (bloody). Sharks are also attracted to fresh blood. So if you're bleeding, don't go in the water. If you cut yourself while you're in the water, get out—fast!

BIG BAD SHARKS

Shark attacks are rare—and those that result in death are even rarer. But here are some that have a killer reputation.

BLACK-TIP SHARK

WHERE IT LIVES: tropical and subtropical waters, plus coral lagoons and mangrove swamps

HOW BIG IS IT? about 5 feet (1.5 m)

WHAT'S FOR DINNER: small schooling fish such as sardines, herring, and anchovies

YIKES: Black-tip sharks will dart through a school of fish, chomp at their meal, then burst through the water's surface and spin around three or four times.

IN CASE YOU WANTED TO KNOW: Scuba divers often encounter black-tips while exploring reefs.

TIGER SHARK

WHERE IT LIVES: worldwide in temperate, tropical, and subtropical waters (except the Mediterranean Sea)

HOW BIG IS IT? average 13 to 16 feet (4 to 5 m) long; largest can be more than 25 feet (8 m)

WHAT'S FOR DINNER: Tiger sharks aren't picky and munch sea turtles, rays, bony fish, sea birds, dolphins, squid, and even other tiger sharks.

YIKES: These guys will furiously shake their heads back and forth to tear chunks from their victims.

IN CASE YOU WANTED TO KNOW: Tiger sharks got their name because of the cool stripes on their bodies.

GREAT WHITE SHARK

WHERE IT LIVES: worldwide in temperate waters; the biggest prefer tropical

HOW BIG IS IT? average 13 to 16 feet (4 to 5 m) long; largest can be more than 22 feet (7 m)

WHAT'S FOR DINNER: pinnipeds like seals and sea lions; dolphins

YIKES: Great whites have about 3,000 three-inch-long (8 cm) teeth at any given time.

IN CASE YOU WANTED TO KNOW: Great whites are the only sharks that will poke their heads out of the water to look around.

BULL SHARK

WHERE IT LIVES: tropical and subtropical oceans and sometimes—gulp—fresh-water

HOW BIG IS IT? 8 to 11 feet (2.4 to 3.4 m) long

WHAT'S FOR DINNER: another one that eats just about anything: bony fishes, smaller sharks, rays, turtles, shrimp, squid, birds, and (yum!) garbage

YIKES: Bull sharks have been spotted more than 1,750 miles (2,816 km) from the mouth of the Mississippi River in Illinois, and more than 2,000 miles (3,219 km) from the mouth of the Amazon River in Peru.

IN CASE YOU WANTED TO KNOW: Bull sharks are speedy, swimming in quick bursts up to 11 miles an hour (18 kph).

SAND TIGER SHARK

WHERE IT LIVES: most warm seas except the eastern Pacific Ocean

HOW BIG IS IT? average 4 to 9 feet (1.2 to 2.7 m) long

WHAT'S FOR DINNER: small bony fish, eels, crustaceans, and maybe an octopus or two

YIKES: Sand tiger sharks have three rows of teeth.

IN CASE YOU WANTED TO KNOW: Sand tigers will gulp air into their stomachs so they can hover motionless in the water…the better to surprise their victims.

HOW TO SURVIVE

A MEAN TEACHER

It seems like no matter what you do, Mr. Eyehateya the math teacher seems to have it in for you. There's no way to survive the semester with a teacher who seems bent on keeping you in middle school till you're 25. Here's how to move yourself from the metaphorical corner to the A-list.

BE THE TEACHER.

Before you conclude that your teacher is simply evil, take a look at things from his or her point of view. Are you late for class? Do you forget to turn in assignments? Talk too much? Text when the teacher is talking? Uh, might be a good idea to stop doing those things and focus on school.

FAKE AN INTEREST.

Maybe you'd rather read the phone book than diagram another sentence, but don't let your teacher know that. Make it look like you care about the subject. Raise your hand to answer questions. (Just make sure you know the answer.) Ask questions about the material. Don't roll your eyes when your teacher hands out homework or springs a pop quiz.

DON'T BE A SUCK-UP.

Participate in class, but don't overdo it. Knowing all the answers will just annoy other students. And a teacher will see right through an overly enthusiastic kid. One too many "Wow, the Monroe Doctrine of 1823 is so interesting—tell us more!" might make your teacher think you're making fun of the topic.

FIND A SURVIVOR.

Let's face it. Some teachers just aren't very nice. Seek out students who've survived this teacher and get their advice. They may have some inside scoop on what really drives the teacher crazy, and what's considered cool behavior. Who knew that humming "Jail House Rock" before class would put the teacher in such a good mood?

GET A ONE-ON-ONE.

Discuss your situation face-to-face with your teacher. After class is over and the other students have left, ask your teacher for some time before or after school or during lunch to meet with you privately. You don't have to be specific, but give some idea of what you want to discuss. "I'd like to talk about how I'm doing in class" is vague yet shows your teacher you're mature enough to discuss a concern.

SURVIVING A TALK WITH YOUR TEACHER

It's up to you to start the conversation, but be mature. Don't make accusations; instead, focus on your concern. "I want to know why you hate me" will only put your teacher on the defensive. "I feel like we've gotten off on the wrong foot" or "I think I've done something to make you mad" will show your teacher you're taking responsibility.

Listen to what your teacher has to say. Don't look at the clock or wave to your friends passing by. Pay attention, nod slowly, and don't interrupt, even if your teacher starts droning on about how things were back in 1972.

Ask what you can do to help improve the situation. Your teacher will definitely have some advice, and now you know exactly what you need to do to stay on his or her good side.

Don't argue with your teacher. Trying to explain that it was your best friend's fault you got caught with a drawing of your teacher with snakes for hair only keeps things in the past. You'll get props from your teacher if you own up to past mistakes and move on.

CHAPTER 16

HOW TO SURVIVE

A SNAKE-BITE

This could be a pretty short chapter, because there's only one way to survive a venomous snakebite: Get to a hospital for a shot of antivenom! But if simply avoiding a snakebite counts as a way to survive, then we've got you covered.

WEAR THE LATEST STYLE.

When walking in snake country, put on thick boots and pants. You may be in for the surprise of your life when a snake attacks your shoe, but think about the surprise the snake's getting when it tries to bite into your stinky footwear.

FIND YOUR PATH.

Stay on clear trails with no overgrowth. Snakes hate it when they're trying to take a nap and someone steps on them.

LOG IN.

Don't just step over logs. Step on top of them and look on the other side. If there's a snake resting against the log, smile politely and slowly back away. And don't put your hand into a hollow log or a crevice without first looking inside.

STEP AWAY FROM THE SNAKE.

A snake isn't lurking in the bushes to eat you. In fact, snakes would rather slither away from you than attack, and they usually only attack when threatened. So don't threaten one! If you come across a snake, stay calm and slowly head in the other direction.

A DEAD SNAKE CAN STILL INJECT VENOM.

DON'T PANIC.

If you are bitten, stay calm. Try to wash the wound and keep it slightly below your heart. Remove rings or bracelets in case you start to swell. If you have a cell phone with service, call for help. (Tell rescuers exactly where you are.) Otherwise walk—don't run—to find help and get to a hospital. Do not apply suction, ice, or a tourniquet, and don't cut the wound.

DEADLY VERSUS PUPPY DOG

Pit vipers are among the deadliest poisonous snakes found throughout the world. Rattlesnakes, moccasins, and bushmasters are a few of the different species in this family. You can distinguish them from harmless snakes, but here's a thought: Don't get up close and personal with any snake you come across. Just leave them all alone. But in case you're wondering, pit vipers usually have:

Vertical pupils slit like a cat's

Dark bands from their eyes to the corner of their jaws

Large, triangle-shaped heads with a narrow neck

Thick, heavy bodies

BEWARE OF SNAKE

BLACK MAMBAS are some of the most feared snakes around, though you won't come across a wild one unless you're in Africa. They're big, reaching up to 14 feet (4.3 m) long. They're fast, slithering along at 12.5 miles an hour (20 kph). And they're deadly: Without antivenom, a bite is 100 percent fatal, usually in about 20 minutes.

AUSTRALIA'S INLAND TAIPAN is believed to have the most poisonous venom of any land snake in the world, with the potential to kill a human in a few hours. According to the Australia Zoo, one bite is toxic enough to kill a hundred men.

THE BUSHMASTER of Central and South America is sort of like a rattlesnake—without the rattle to warn you away. Known to be able to kill a human within an hour, this snake will stake out one spot for several weeks waiting for prey. But if it eases your mind at all—it's only after small rodents...usually.

THE EASTERN DIAMONDBACK RATTLESNAKE is the largest venomous snake in North America. It's also the most polite. If one's about to strike, it'll let you know with the telltale buzzing sound of its rattle. Then watch out—the eastern diamondback can accurately strike at up to one-third its body length.

CHAPTER 17

HOW TO SURVIVE

GOSSIP

P *ssst!* Did you hear about how you got sent to the principal's office four times last week? Apparently you've been passing notes in all your classes, giving your teachers nicknames like Mr. Fartsalot and Mrs. Snoozerson. Everyone knows you wrote them, so of course you're in *sooo* much trouble. Great story—except it's not true. Try the tips on the next page to silence the gossipmongers.

FOLLOW THE CHAIN.

Instead of feeling your brain explode when you first hear what you've apparently done, ask your friends who they heard it from. Then ask those people where they heard it, and so on and so on till you find the Big Mouth.

POINT THE FINGER.

When you figure out who tattled the tale, let that person know that you know, and ask for an explanation. Big Mouth may deny it, but at least the kid knows that you're on to him and will probably zip those lips.

HAVE STORYTIME.

Most rumors have a tiny grain of truth to them. For instance, you may not be passing notes, but perhaps you did make up a mean name for a teacher the same week you got called out of class early to go to a doctor's appointment. It's just that somehow those things turned you into The Kid Most Likely to Spend Summer Vacation in Detention, according to Nosy McGossippants. So tell your side of the story and get the actual facts out there.

DENY, DENY, DENY.

If the rumor is so not true—not even a little bit—stand up for yourself and let people know. But don't rant and rave, go on and on, yell, scream, or cry. You'll look like you're trying too hard, which will make you look guilty for sure.

THEN WAIT IT OUT.

Gossip is like an invisible bully. The more you show it bothers you, the more it'll kick your butt. Ignore the whispers, and they'll eventually fade away.

ARE YOU THE GOSSIP?

1.
You've just seen the kid in the leather biker jacket head into the principal's office. You:

A. Press your ear against the door to get the scoop.

B. Tell your BFF what you saw.

C. Move along.

2.
A friend gives you the scoop that your math teacher has the hots for the lunch lady. You:

A. Tell your friend why you think that might be true.

B. Make a gagging sound when you think about old people dating.

C. Change the subject and start guessing what the "secret ingredient" in the cafeteria's burgers really is.

3.
A teammate has just beaten you in the 50-yard dash. You:

A. Congratulate your teammate.

B. Start psyching yourself up for the next race.

C. Tell the rest of your team that the kid's mom pays for a private coach.

ANSWERS: You might be a gossip if you answered 1. B, 2. A, 3. C.

95

CHAPTER 18

HOW TO SURVIVE

A KILLER BEE ATTACK

That buzzing sound may not be the result of too many energy drinks. If the sky has suddenly turned dark, it may be killer bees. The good news? These little killers can only sting once before they die. The bad news? They can swarm in groups of hundreds. One sting times hundreds of bees equals a sure-fire trip to the emergency room. Here's what to do when the latest buzz is definitely not cool.

BUZZ OFF.

Killer bees aren't out to get you. They only attack when they think their hive is being threatened. If you see several bees buzzing near you, a hive is probably close by. Heed their "back off" attitude and slowly walk away.

DON'T JOIN THE SWAT TEAM.

Your first instinct might be to start swatting and slapping the bees. But that just makes the buzzers think you're King Kong trying to destroy New York City. Loud noises have the same effect, so don't start screaming and treating the bees like they're Whac-A-Moles. Just get away.

DON'T PLAY HIDE-AND-SEEK.

Hives are often near water, but don't even think about outlasting the bees underwater. They'll hover and attack when you come up for air, even if you try to swim for it.

MAKE LIKE SPEEDY GONZALES.

Killer bees will chase you, but they'll give up when you're far enough away from the hive (usually about 200 yards [183 m]). Take off as if Freddy Krueger wants to introduce you to his fingernails, and don't stop till the buzzing does.

CREATE A COVER-UP.

Killer bees often go for the face and throat, which are the most dangerous places to be stung. While you're on the run, protect your face and neck with your hands, or pull your shirt over your head. You may look a little silly, but it's better than ending up looking like Pumpkinhead.

MYTH BUSTED!

A killer bee, also known as an Africanized honeybee, is no more potent than a regular honeybee. What gives these bees their deadly nickname is their aggressive nature. They react much faster to perceived threats and attack in far greater numbers. Some scientists estimate that a swarm of killer bees will sting ten times as often as a swarm of regular honeybees.

HOW TO SURVIVE A BEE STING

Get inside or to a cool place.

Get the stinger out by scraping a fingernail over the area, like you would to get a splinter out. Do not squeeze the stinger or use tweezers unless you absolutely can't get it out any other way.

Wash the area with soap and water, and apply a cold compress to reduce swelling.

Continue icing the spot for 20 minutes every hour. Place a washcloth or towel between the ice and your skin.

With a parent's permission, take an antihistamine and gently rub a hydrocortisone cream on the sting site.

Don't scratch the area. This will just increase the pain and swelling.

If you experience severe burning and itching, swelling of the throat and/or mouth, difficulty breathing, weakness, or nausea, or if you already know you are allergic to bees, get to an emergency room immediately.

OTHER BUGS THAT CAN KILL YOU (BUT DON'T WORRY— THEY USUALLY DON'T)

SYDNEY FUNNEL-WEB SPIDER:

There's nothing worse than grabbing a shirt off the floor and finding out a spider's been living under your dirty laundry. (Oh. *That's* why Mom is always nagging you!) Except maybe discovering a Sydney funnel-web spider under your clothes. These Australian natives can be as big as a human adult's palm and show no fear—they'll grab you and bite several times with superlong fangs. Without treatment, you're a goner in an hour. Luckily, treatment is readily available, and you shouldn't come across these guys unless you're in Sydney, Australia.

SCORPION:

That's right. Scorpions may look like stinging lobsters but they're actually arachnids, like spiders. Even though most scorpion stings will only make you bawl like a baby, about 25 of the approximately 1,500 species of scorpions are deadly. These killers reside all over the world but usually don't do fatal damage unless you're a little kid or super old. One with a *really* bad rep is the death stalker of Africa and the Middle East. It has extremely potent venom and kills several people a year.

KILLER CATERPILLAR:

If you see a fuzzy caterpillar in Brazil, stay far, far away. *Lonomia oblique* has spiny hairs that inject poison by just brushing up against something (like your arm). The poison stops your blood from clotting, which means that you start bleeding—everywhere. But it doesn't stay deadly for long: The caterpillar will eventually turn into a harmless butterfly.

MOSQUITO:
You may think that the most harm a mosquito can do is make you itch like crazy. But actually, they can carry serious diseases such as deadly malaria, yellow and dengue fevers, and encephalitis. Even though drugs that will treat malaria are readily available, the disease kills more than one million people every year, mostly in Africa. Some scientists say that mosquitos have killed more people than all the wars in history.

CHAPTER 19

HOW TO SURVIVE

THE INTERNET

Seems like you can't get away from adults telling you what to do. Parents are constantly nagging you to quit texting or to take out the trash. Teachers are always on your back to study more. Even your coach seems to get a maniacal thrill out of watching you collapse in exhaustion.

No wonder the Internet can be an escape. It's the one place where you have freedom and independence. You can hang with your friends, act however you want, meet cool people, and explore places you've never been—with minimal adult supervision. But just like in the real world, you have to be smart in the online world.

ACT LIKE A MOVIE STAR.

You can bet that Johnny Depp never gives out his phone number, address, Social Security number, birthdate, password, or any personal details to people who aren't his closest friends and family. Movie stars guard their privacy, and on the Internet, you should, too. There's never a reason for people you know only online to have personal information. If they ask for things like your full name, email address, where you go to school, your town, where your parents work, even if you're a boy or a girl, something's probably up.

THERE'S FRIENDS...AND THEN THERE'S FRIENDS.

Admit it...sometimes when you're online you pretend to be a little older than you actually are, or to love a movie you secretly hated to impress someone. Lots of people do a little self-improvement on the Internet, but it's when people take it to the extreme that it can get dangerous. So be cautious of online friends who you don't know in real life, and remember that anyone can be anything on the Internet. The student body president at the school across town who says he wants your email address so he can send you a picture may be a computer hacker trying to forward you a virus that will turn your computer's hard drive into a pile of goo. That cheerleader who wants to know where you'll be after school could be a pirate looking to kidnap teenagers for ransom to fund his stuffed animal collection. (OK, that's probably unlikely. But you get the point.)

Give us all your information, we'll give you $1,000!

Sign me up!

BE A MYSTERY MAN (OR LADY).

Keep your screen name impersonal so that people you don't know can't figure out personal details like where you go to school, your gender, or your age. QTgrl98 and musclboi12 are not the best choices.

BRING A BODYGUARD.

You're no dummy: You're playing it safe by meeting an online friend for the first time at the mall with a group of pals. And when he doesn't show up, you just figure something came up. No worries, right? Except that "friend" was there all along…he was that bald guy with the bad teeth standing in line at the Chinese takeout place. And when you and your friends left, he followed you home. So just suck it up and have a parent go with you when you're meeting someone for the first time—when a bad guy sees that you've got an adult looking out for you, he'll more than likely stay far away.

YOU HAVE NOT JUST WON A MILLION DOLLARS.

It can be hard to tell if something's a scam. But just like in real life, if something seems too good to be true, then it probably is. Never trade personal information for free stuff. No one is trying to find you to give you money from a long-lost cousin. You have not won a fabulous trip to the Bahamas. You will not receive $5,000 for sending a dollar to four people on a list.

PURGE JUNK MAIL.

Don't open any emails or attachments from someone you don't know. They could contain spyware that will allow the sender to collect information about you without your knowledge (do you really want everyone to know you have iheartclowns. com bookmarked?), viruses that will eat that science fair project you've been working on for weeks, or photos of your teacher in roller skates and knee socks (and who wants to see *that*?).

SMART SHOPPING.

Make sure any purchases you make are from reputable sites, like online stores for businesses you can actually walk into. Check out user reviews for sites like eBay; they don't have a lot of monitoring, and scam artists often prey on unsuspecting shoppers.

PUT ON SUNGLASSES AND AN EARPIECE.

Your password should be as impossible to decode as the White House's security system; otherwise, someone could figure it out, log on, and pretend to be you. (Identity theft aside—it's the $5,000 worth of iTunes downloads you may have to explain to your parent.) Your birthday, school mascot, pet's name, street names, and even colors are supereasy to figure out, so use weird combinations of letters and numbers, and change it often. Keep it somewhere safe—and by safe we mean someplace other than a sticky note on your computer.

GET SOME PRIVACY.

Want that weirdo living in a houseboat off the coast of Madagascar to see your photos of you and your friends at the end-of-the-school-year picnic? Didn't think so. Set your privacy settings on social networking sites so that only your friends have access to your page.

DO A CREDIT CHECK.

OK, so you've never heard of this guy, but his online profile says he's friends with eight of your buds. He's probably OK, right? Don't count on it. Make sure you know who you're friending before allowing him access to your site. Same goes for responding to IMs or emails. If you've never heard of the sender, check her out with other real friends.

OH, BE-HAVE!

Sometimes the biggest danger on the Internet is… *you!* It's easy to forget how public the online world really is, so be careful how you act.

If you wouldn't say it in person, don't say it online. You'll probably regret it later, plus someone may use your comment against you one day. Even worse: Unacceptable online behavior could get you in trouble at school or kicked out of clubs or teams.

Today that picture of you smooching your Justin Bieber poster is totally hilarious, but a year from now you may cringe with embarrassment. Don't post photos that you wouldn't want your grandmother, teacher, or secret crush seeing.

Remember, nothing is temporary on the Internet. Even stuff you delete—embarrassing postings of you dissing your best friend, videos of you crashing your bike after jumping a ramp made out of cereal boxes—can be retrieved. Or they may have been copied or downloaded by other people and could come back to haunt you. The best advice? Think about what you post *before* you put it out there for everyone to see.

Google yourself. If you're trying to land a babysitting or lawn-mowing gig, get into a private school, or be accepted by an exclusive club, you can be sure that those people are Googling you. They are *not* going to be impressed with the death-to-puppy-dog lyrics you wrote as a joke or the photo of you TPing your neighbor's yard. See what the Internet has to say about you, and see if you can have anything embarrassing deleted.

SPEAK UP!

If you receive any inappropriate or offensive material online, don't delete it. Tell an adult, then report it to cybertipline.org, a service from the National Center for Missing and Exploited Children. The information will be forwarded to law enforcement agencies for investigation and reported to the service provider, if possible. **107**

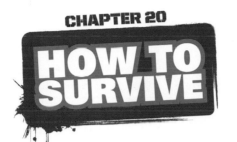

CHAPTER 20

HOW TO SURVIVE

AN ALLIGATOR OR CROCODILE ATTACK

When you're hanging out in the ocean, you know you gotta worry about sharks or being swept out to sea. But having to fret about ending up as the lunch special on a saltwater crocodile's menu? *Really?* Come on!

The fact is, all of the above are incredibly unlikely. But though they live primarily on land, saltwater crocodiles have been spotted hunting far out at sea. Like their cousin Al (as in alligator), these guys are superpredators that eat pretty much whatever they want, whenever they want. Read on to find out how to avoid becoming dinner.

STAY AWAY. STAY FAR, FAR AWAY.

Like, 50 feet (15 m) away if you see an alligator or a crocodile, especially if it's in the water. A gator can swim up to 20 miles an hour (32 kph), and both have powerful tails that propel them out of the water to grab prey.

JOIN THE TRACK TEAM.

As in, run. As fast as you can. Gators and crocs may be Olympic swimmers in the water, but on land their stumpy legs don't take them very far. Alligators *can* sprint at about 10 miles an hour (16 kph), but they'll give up long before you break a sweat.

PRETEND YOU'RE ON FIRE.

You know that advice, Stop, drop, and roll? The croc or alligator will take care of those steps for you. Their killing method is to clamp down and roll victims in the water till they drown. It sounds weird, but if a gator or croc grabs you, try to roll with it; otherwise you might break a limb.

WARNING ALLIGATORS

NO SWIMMING

KEEP ROLLING...WITH SOME PUNCHES.

Alligators are especially lazy and don't want to work too hard for their meals. Crocodiles are more aggressive, but if you suddenly find yourself between two rows of sharp teeth, fight back. Jab a finger into its eye. Punch or kick its snout or ears. A smart alligator knows that no meal is worth that kind of fight, so hopefully it'll open its jaws enough to allow your escape.

CHOMP!

Because of the large number of people who live near rivers where Nile crocodiles live, it's estimated that about 200 people a year die from injuries caused by these hungry predators.

Even if the attack leaves just a flesh wound, get to a hospital for treatment. Alligators have bacteria in their saliva that can cause serious—sometimes deadly—infections. What's the point of surviving a gator attack only to die from its spit?

PARENTING 101

Despite being such scary predators, alligators and crocodiles are great parents. Both mom and dad Nile crocodiles guard the nest and will often gently roll the eggs in their mouths to help them hatch. When croc and gator babies are threatened, moms will call them to swim into their mouths to hide. And they're not just kicked out of the nest: Alligator and crocodile babies stay with Mom until they're about two years old.

THE ALLIGATOR SPECIES IS 150 MILLION YEARS OLD; IT SURVIVED WHATEVER KILLED THE DINOSAURS.

WHAT'S THE DIFF?

You should be able to figure out if it's an alligator or crocodile depending on where you are (see pages 112-113), but just in case you've landed in the middle of your worst nightmare where the two coexist, there are physical differences, too.

ALLIGATORS have wide, rounded snouts, and you can't see their teeth when their jaws are closed.

CROCODILES have narrow, pointier snouts, and the fourth tooth of their lower jaw sticks up over the upper lip.

ALLIGATOR-CROCODILE SMACKDOWN

SALTWATER CROCODILE

RANGE: Australia, India, China, Southeast Asia

LENGTH: average 17 feet, but up to 23 feet (5 to 7 m) is not uncommon

WEIGHT: average 1,000 pounds (454 kg), but you might see some over 2,000 pounds (907 kg), too

CRAVES: pretty much what alligators like, plus water buffalo, monkeys, wild boars, sharks

NILE CROCODILE

RANGE: sub-Saharan Africa, Nile Basin, Madagascar

LENGTH: up to 20 feet (6 m)

WEIGHT: 500-1,650 pounds (227 to 748 kg)

CRAVES: mostly fish, but crocs aren't picky: zebras, small hippos, wildebeest, and other crocodiles are all on the menu

AMERICAN ALLIGATOR

RANGE: southeastern United States, from North Carolina to Texas (most are in Florida and Louisiana)

LENGTH: up to 15 feet (4.6 m)

WEIGHT: up to 1,000 pounds (454 kg)

CRAVES: fish, turtles, snakes, the occasional deer and wild pig, and other small animals (including Fido)

DON'T FEED THE ALLIGATORS

Be smart if you're in alligator or crocodile country to avoid provoking an attack.

Make them find their own dinner. Just like the title says: Don't feed them. For one thing, it's illegal in most places. Plus alligators and crocodiles that associate humans with food are more likely to attack—whether you brought snacks or not.

Follow the rules. If there's a sign posted outside a swimming area warning of crocs or gators, don't swim there!

The sun is your friend. If you're in gator / crocland, swim when the sun is high. Dusk and dawn are when they like to hunt.

Stay back. Avoid walking too close to the water's edge where alligators and crocs are known to hunt. That's where they hide to catch lunch.

Beware of cloudy water. Alligators and crocs are sneaky; they hide underwater with just their eyes above the surface so they can stealthily stalk prey. Cloudy, murky water only adds to their ninja style. So swim in clear water, where the banks aren't overgrown with brush or weeds.

Be nice. Like we said, crocodiles are much more aggressive, but alligators tend to attack humans when provoked. So don't try to capture a baby for a pet; big mama is probably nearby and will be seriously peeved. (And that cute baby gator is going to grow into a mean, green, eating machine.) Don't tease a gator by throwing sticks or rocks. Steer clear of any gator during early to mid-summer, otherwise known as mating season.

HOW TO SURVIVE
UNCHARTERED TERRITORY

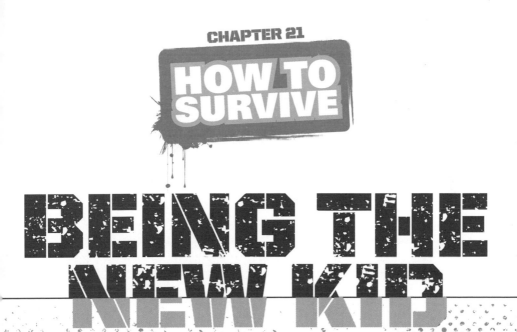

CHAPTER 21

HOW TO SURVIVE

BEING THE NEW KID

Starting a new school sounds about as much fun as diving into a swimming pool filled with three-month-old, broccoli-flavored yogurt: confusing, terrifying, and a little bit nauseating.

But look at it this way: You're the *new* kid. People will be curious about what you're all about. Plus, they'll have no idea that you accidentally blew up the science lab or hung out in the teachers' lounge at your old school. You can be anything you want now. Check out the tips in this chapter to get the most out of your mystery status.

WHAT I DID ON MY SUMMER VACATION.

If you've moved before school starts, check out summer stuff—art classes, sports teams, even the local pool. It's a great way to meet people before classes begin. (Practicing your disco dance moves in your front yard is probably not going to attract a lot of new friends.)

GO ON TOUR.

Try to tour the school before your first day. Find your classrooms, your locker, the cafeteria, and the bathrooms. Wiggling in your seat to avoid an "accident" in the middle of science class is *not* the way to get noticed.

YOU ARE HERE

DRESS FOR SUCCESS.

No matter what adults say, *you* know that some classmates will judge you based on how you look. No one's asking you to show up looking like you're about to shoot a music video. Just look nice, and wear what makes you feel confident. At the very least, comb your hair.

CHINA HAS THE LONGEST SCHOOL YEAR OF ANY COUNTRY.

GO CLUBBING.

Join a couple of clubs or a sports team, especially if you did the same activities at your old school. You'll meet people with the same interests and have an instant group to hang out with.

KEEP SMILING.

You don't want people to think you've been locked in a basement your whole life. Appear friendly and approachable—even if you're shy by nature or secretly terrified.

SAFETY IN NUMBERS.

Chances are, you're not the only new kid in school, and the others are just as terrified as you are. So seek out other newbies and say hi. Ask about where they're from. You can commiserate over that weird smell in the cafeteria.

SNEAK ATTACK.

Most kids already have friends, so it's going to be up to you to break the ice. Start small: Ask for directions to your next class, tell them you like their sunglasses, or see if they have any info about the teacher.

BECOME A LOCAL.

People always complain about how *booorrrinnnggg* their town or school is, but they don't want *you* to do that until you've been there a while. That goes double if you're comparing stuff to your old town. So steer clear of negative talk and get interested in what there is to do in your new town. Ask them about the best places to hang.

119

HOW TO SURVIVE ANYTHING

MAKE THE FIRST MOVE.

Now that you're friendly with a few people, be the one to ask them to see a movie or come over and study. Pretty soon they'll start asking you to do stuff, too.

SAY HEY.

Once you start recognizing people, say hello whenever you see them, like in the hallways or cafeteria. And use their names. This lets people know you are friendly and outgoing. Just don't make a scene: Jumping up and down, waving your arms, and screaming till they acknowledge you is *not* cool.

NO SMOTHERING, PLEASE.

So now you have a friend or two. Be cool about it. Don't ask if they want to hang out every day. Don't text them every 11 minutes. Don't post on their Facebook wall every time you hear the song that was playing the day you met. No one wants a clingy friend.

SAY THIS

- ◎ "Cool shoes."
- ◎ "Have you seen that piano-playing cat on YouTube?"
- ◎ "Where's the best place to get cupcakes in this town?"
- ◎ "Can I borrow your pen for a sec?"
- ◎ "Are you going to the game Friday?"

NOT THAT

- ◎ "Man, I am *so* tired. My mom threw out my Wubie and I can't sleep without it."
- ◎ "Want to come over and see my scrapbook about how awesome I am?"
- ◎ "I hate pandas and kittens."
- ◎ "I think boogers taste great."
- ◎ "All our problems would be solved if Homer Simpson were President."

HOW TO SURVIVE THE FIRST DAY OF MIDDLE SCHOOL

Get the scoop on teachers. Maybe your big brother will let you out of a headlock long enough to give you some hints on how to deal. If not, see if any of your friends' older siblings can help.

You don't want to be standing outside picking your nose all by yourself on the first day of school. A few days before, call your friends and arrange a meet-up spot before school so you're not totally alone. (Better to pick your nose with some friends!)

Memorize your locker combination.

Try to explore the school before the first day to figure out your class-to-class route.

Surviving the first day is much easier if you know what to expect. Go over your schedule with all your buds to see who's in your classes. Even if you'll be flying solo in some classes, just having that info will keep you from feeling like you're waiting for a stay of execution before the bell rings.

Pack your lunch the night before. If you're buying, make sure you've stashed some cash.

Stock your backpack the day before with everything you might need.

Plan your wardrobe. Double-check the dress code, and wear something you *know* you look good in. Don't dress to impress—that new sweater may be *the* coolest thing in your closet, but if it's hot outside you'll look ridiculous.

DVR those late-night reruns and get some sleep.

Eat breakfast. No one wants to hear your stomach participate in a classroom discussion.

121

CHAPTER 22

HOW TO SURVIVE

FALLING THROUGH ICE

Taking that shortcut across the frozen lake *seems* like the right thing to do. That is, until the ice starts cracking and you realize you're about to become a frozen fish stick. It's too late for a lecture on how you never should have been out on the ice in the first place, so here's a plan to thaw you out:

CALM AND COLD.

This ain't like splashing water on your face to wake yourself up. This water is so cold that it literally takes your breath away. Take long, deep breaths to get your breathing under control. Calmly tread water instead of splashing around, which will only tire you out and make breathing more difficult.

WHIP IT AROUND.

Face the direction from where you came. The ice was strong enough to hold you for a while, so that's where you want to escape to. Snap off thin ice until you get to a thickness that will support your weight.

FIND YOUR ANIMAL INSTINCT.

You have about ten minutes before you lose all feeling in your arms and legs and are able to move about as well as a newly wrapped mummy, so move fast. Place your arms palms-down on the ice and try to shimmy your torso like a walrus onto the surface. Kick your legs like a dolphin and pull your body forward to propel yourself out of the water. Do *not* try to push yourself out of the water as if you were hoisting yourself out of the pool with your hands. This will put too much weight on the ice and break it more.

CREATE A LOGJAM.

Once you're out of the water, do not stand up unless you want to fall right through the ice again. (We're guessing not.) Instead, roll your way to shore. You may look like a giant snowball, but it's better than being a giant Popsicle.

BRING ON THE HOT CHOCOLATE.

Get out of those wet clothes, wrap yourself in your favorite blankie, and sip (as in don't gulp) a warm (as in not hot) beverage.

STILL STANDING?

What's more stupid than one person walking on a frozen river? *Two* people walking on a frozen river. If you see someone fall through the ice, here's what to do.

Well, here's what *not* to do. Do *not* rush to the hole and try to pull the person out. You'll either fall through yourself, or your panicky friend will just pull you in. (I mean, you're close, but you don't want to be *that* close.) Instead, immediately call 9-1-1, or ask someone else to go get help.

Extend a ski, a rope, a branch—anything grabbable—from the shore. Try to pull your friend out, but if *you* start to get pulled in, let go.

Try to help your friend to get out using the instructions on this page. Talk through the steps.

If you have a rope, tell your friend to tie it around his or her waist. Or tie one end in a circle, then have the person loop it over her elbows, her hands touching her shoulders. This way if your friend gets too weak to hold on to anything, rescuers can still do their job.

From a safe distance (and by safe distance, we mean the shore), talk to your friend. Calmly say that help is on the way and that things are going to be all right. You may not be so sure, but your friend needs to hear that to stay calm.

Make sure to get your friend warm and dry as soon as possible, and get to a hospital.

KNOW THE SNOW

It's nearly impossible to guess how thick ice is. Lots of things—temperature, age, water depth, size, currents, even fish swimming underneath—affect the thickness. And don't be fooled by snow on top of ice. The snow can be like a warm blanket and melt the ice underneath. Bottom line: Don't walk on outdoor ice unless it's a skating rink!

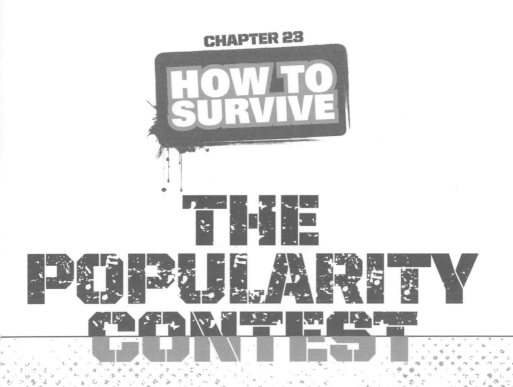

CHAPTER 23

HOW TO SURVIVE

THE POPULARITY CONTEST

So you may not have six pairs of the latest jeans or score five touchdowns a game. Popularity doesn't mean you have to constantly be surrounded by an entourage. *True* popularity means having friends who make you happy. When you have a reputation as a nice person who people like, you don't need a guaranteed seat at the "cool table." You'll be having too much fun with all your friends to care where anyone's sitting. Here are a few tips that will help you find (and keep) your BFFs.

STEP ONE: FIND FRIENDS

Drama Club Sign-up

BE A JOINER.

It's easy to make friends with people who have the same interests as you. School clubs are great, but look beyond your locker. Check out your local community centers, museums, zoos, and parks and recreation department for cool activities. If you can't tell the difference between a baseball and a football, look for noncompetitive sports teams, like kickball or flag football.

FIND YOUR INNER SUPERHERO.

Teach little kids how to read, clean out some cages at an animal shelter, or entertain at a nursing home. Volunteering is a great way to meet people, plus there's no better conversation than one between two people saving the world.

START YOUR OWN GROUP.

The best groups are ones in which the members are actually friends and have similar interests. Ask your teacher if you can pass around a sign-up sheet for a study group. Form your own rock band, book club, or hiking group. Make your meetings fun: Hold them away from school, have everyone bring snacks, and don't feel like you have to stick to an agenda. Sometimes it's better to *act* like Tom Sawyer than to discuss him for an hour. (But remember, just because someone isn't part of your group doesn't mean you can't be friends.)

STEP TWO: MAKE FRIENDS

▶ START THE CONVERSATION.

It's easy to start a pressure-free conversation with a potential friend.

◎ Make a simple comment or offer a compliment, like "That test was a killer," or "I love your sweater."

◎ When the person responds, ask a question that requires more than a yes-or-no answer. "How much did you have to study for the test?" or "Where did you get that sweater?"

◎ As the conversation moves forward, talk about things you have in common: a little brother, math class, your goal to be a gazillionaire by the time you're 20.

◎ React to what the other person is saying: "Oh my gosh, she did *not* say that!" or "Dude, I totally know what you mean."

◎ Keep asking questions to show you're interested in what the other person has to say.

◎ Make eye contact. Smile. Laugh every once in a while. If you look unfriendly or bored, people will *think* you're unfriendly or bored.

◎ Stay in the conversation. Don't text, check email, or take calls on your phone.

◎ If this is a brand-new person, introduce yourself toward the end. "By the way, my name is Madonna." (Substitute your real name.) The other person will do the same.

◎ End the conversation with "It was nice talking with you, Elvis." (Again, use real names.)

◎ Next time you see your new friend, use his (real) name. "Hey, Barack." (Insert small head nod here.)

START A COLLECTION.

Once you've said hello a couple times to the skateboarder in your English class, make the first move and suggest that you hang out. You might just see a movie together, or perhaps your new friend can teach you to ride without falling on your butt.

GET THE PARTY STARTED.

Getting different sets of friends together is a great way to build a group. Have a party to introduce people. They'll see you as "that kid who has those great friends" and will like you even more.

STEP THREE: KEEP FRIENDS

Take this quiz to see how friend-worthy you are.

QUESTION 1

You're supposed to meet a friend at the movies, but you got sidetracked playing video games. You:

A. Keep playing video games; the movie's already started anyway.

B. Call your friend to say you're running late but you're on your way.

C. Tell your friend to meet you at your house instead to play more video games.

D. Hop on your bike and pedal as fast as you can to the theater—your friend will probably wait for you.

Answer: B.—this one time only. A good friend is reliable and doesn't make excuses.

QUESTION 2

You and your bestie are talking about the cutie your BF met at summer camp. You:

A. Ask if they're planning to meet up.

B. Start raving about a cutie *you* met at summer camp.

C. Tell your friend to forget it—long-distance things never work.

D. Get online to post about your friend's crush.

Answer: A. A good friend is supportive and a good listener, and doesn't try to top another friend's story.

QUESTION 3

You and a friend are about to head to a pool party when the parental units call to inform your bud that there's a yardful of leaves waiting to be raked at home. You:

A. Tell your friend to blow off the 'rents and go to the party anyway.

B. Go to the party solo.

C. Make plans to meet up later.

D. Help your friend rake leaves so you can both get to the party later.

Answer: D. A good friend sometimes makes a sacrifice to help someone out.

QUESTION 4

A popular kid has asked you—but not your BFFs—to sit at the "cool table" in the cafeteria. You:

A. Sit with the cool kids but go on and on about how great your friends are.

B. Tell your friends you'll sit with them tomorrow.

C. Bring your friends with you whether they're invited or not.

D. Don't make eye contact with your BFFs as you pass their table and sit with the other kids.

Answer: C. A good friend never dumps BFFs for the popular crowd.

aire Club Sign-up

CHAPTER 24

HOW TO SURVIVE

A WILDFIRE

A forest fire is *not* the time to whip out some marshmallows and start singing campfire songs like "Do Your Ears Hang Low?" Depending on conditions such as wind and dryness, a forest fire can chase you at more than 6 miles an hour (9.7 kph). (A grassland fire can spread up to *14* miles an hour [23 kph].) So if you're smelling smoke, starting to sweat, and watching rabbits flee like Elmer Fudd is on their tail, it's time to follow the tips in this chapter so you don't become a crispy critter.

FOREST FIRES CAN TRAVEL FASTER UPHILL THAN DOWNHILL.

THE *DUH* FACTOR.

This is obvious, but we gotta say it. The following tips are to be used only if a raging fire is right on top of you. If it's not, just get out of the way—fast.

STARVE THE FIRE.

Fire needs fuel—such as brush, trees, and grass—to burn. So get to a sparse spot without all that clutter, like a road, trail, or empty patch of ground. Stay away from canyons or gulleys. The fire is not an athlete—it will not simply jump over them.

STRIP.

Take off anything polyester, nylon, or rayon. Natural fibers like wool and cotton can protect your skin, but synthetics will just melt. If you're in doubt, strip down to your birthday suit. It's way less painful than getting caught with melted underpants.

EAT A DIRT SANDWICH.

If it's not possible to outrun the flames, lie facedown on the ground and press your nose and mouth into the earth. If you have a cotton or wool blanket, cover yourself with it. At the very least, cover your neck with your shirt, denim jacket, dirt—anything to protect it from the heat.

STAY DOWN.

Remain still and don't get up until the fire is completely over. Inhaling superheated air will *not* make your lungs happy.

BURNING DOWN
THE HOUSE

As land becomes more scarce, cities and suburbs are expanding into once-wild areas that were formerly only inhabited by prison escapees and weird dudes with three-foot-long beards. One result is that forest fires now cause more residential damage than ever. Here's what to do if a fire is knocking at your door.

Get out! Don't wait around to see if the fire changes its mind and heads in another direction. Pack up your pets and grab your parents, it's time they drive you to safety.

Leave the front door unlocked. It's doubtful anyone's going to hang around in a wildfire to steal your mom's spoon collection, and this gives firefighters easy access to protect your house.

Leave a light on in every room. We know, this goes against every single Earth Day tip you've ever heard. But this makes it easier for firefighters to see your house in heavy smoke. The Earth will forgive you—just this once.

ROAD TRIP

Escaping a fire in your car is way more serious than taking a family road trip.

◉ Roll up all the windows and close the air vents.

◉ Drive slowly, and don't drive through heavy smoke.

◉ If it's too dangerous to drive, try to park away from vegetation, turn off the engine, and leave the headlights on.

◉ Have everyone cover themselves and hit the floor. Who knows? You may find that missing CD underneath the driver's seat.

80 PERCENT OF ALL WILDFIRES ARE STARTED BY PEOPLE.

135

CHAPTER 25

HOW TO SURVIVE

THROWING A PARTY

What's better than talking about the awesome party you went to over the weekend? Listening to people talk about the awesome party at *your* house over the weekend! Here's how you can throw the social event everyone will be talking about Monday:

CALM DOWN YOUR PARENTS.

Involve Mom and Dad from the very beginning. Talk with them about a budget, how many people you can invite, and how late the party can go. The more involved they are *before* the party, the less involved they'll have to be *during* the party.

ON AVERAGE, YOU SHARE YOUR BIRTHDAY WITH 1/365th OF THE POPULATION.

SET THE DATE.

Of course you'll want your party on a Friday or Saturday night, but make sure it's not over a holiday weekend or on the night of a big concert or school event. That is, unless you want your guest list to be just you, your little sister, and her stuffed animals.

SPACE IT OUT.

A good rule is to give each guest about four to five square feet of room, so make sure you have a big enough space for all your guests. (Don't forget, you can rearrange furniture or move smaller items out of the room for more space.) Keep in mind that about a third of the people you invite won't come, but some guests will bring friends you didn't invite.

SPREAD THE WORD.

Sending out invitations too close to the date may mean that a lot of your guests will already have plans, so invite people at least two weeks before your party. (Three weeks is even better.) Include the date, the time, and the place, and give guests a date by which to tell you if they're coming or not.

BUG YOUR GUESTS.

Yes, it's totally rude for guests not to let you know if they're coming. But more important, it makes it harder for you to figure out how much food and drinks you'll need. Send an individual reminder to people who haven't responded to your invitation. Make it funny so they don't think you're riding them: "Just want to make sure I have enough food so we don't have to start eating my mom's frozen diet dinners. So let me know if you're coming!"

BREAK THE SILENCE.

There's nothing worse than a party that sounds like it's happening at a library. Create a party mix on your iPod and hook it up to speakers. Pick music with a lot of energy. Include hits your friends love as well as stuff they may not be familiar with. Just don't crank it too high; you don't want your friends to have to scream at each other, and you sure don't want the neighbors complaining.

TRASH IT.

Disposable cups and plates make cleanup a snap. Have big trash bags open in the kitchen so you can dump empties throughout the evening to avoid a big garbage job later.

LOCK UP YOUR SIBLINGS.

Or maybe just ask your parents to keep them busy so they're not annoying you during the party. See if they can spend the night at a friend's or hang out in front of your parents' TV. If they're old enough, you could even hire them as "waiters" to fill drinks and pass out food. (Ten cents an hour? That sounds fair.)

CLEAN YOUR ROOM.

Or at least shut the door. Close off any areas in your house where you don't want guests to wander. This does *not* get you out of cleaning the main party space and the bathroom.

> ### FEED THE ANIMALS.
>
> A couple days before, buy the food and drinks. Keep it simple: chips and dip, candy, cookies, pizza (cut it into bite-size pieces), and sodas. Put most of the food in one place, like a dining room table that guests can walk all the way around. (This prevents traffic jams.) Put a few smaller food bowls around the party space so folks can nosh easily.

GREEN YOUR PARTY

- Shop with reusable bags when buying supplies.
- Buy in bulk to reduce packaging.
- Look for organic snacks and beverages.
- Email invitations to cut down on paper.
- Offer soda in aluminum cans instead of plastic bottles for easier recycling.
- Instead of buying bottled water, fill a pitcher with filtered tap water.
- Use supplies made of recycled materials.
- Buy fun reusable glasses that you can personalize with guests' names. They can take them home as party favors, and you cut down on trash.
- Dim the lights to save electricity. Replace regular lightbulbs with compact fluorescent bulbs or LEDs.
- Set up a recycling center in your kitchen, with separate garbage bags for aluminum, glass, compost, and trash.

HOST WITH THE MOST

Say "Hey" to your guests as soon as they arrive. Don't make them fight through a crowd to find you.

Put out the food and drinks about 30 minutes before the party is supposed to start. Don't panic if people aren't there right on time—it doesn't mean no one's coming. Most people start showing up about 20 minutes after the start time.

Have a designated area where people can throw their coats.

Try to talk to everyone, but don't spend too much time with one person.

Be on the lookout for guests who may not know a lot of people, and make them feel welcome. Introduce them to friends, and get the conversation started. Lines like "Aren't you both Lady Gaga fans?" or "Didn't you spend your summer in Italy? What was that like?" break the ice.

Make sure there's always plenty to eat and drink. Once the food is gone, people will start to leave.

Hang up the phone unless it's a guest calling with a question. Then get back to your guests.

Relax! If you look tired and stressed, your guests won't enjoy themselves. It's a party! Everyone—including the host—is supposed to have a good time.

Try to say goodbye to everyone as they leave, and thank them for coming.

CHAPTER 26

HOW TO SURVIVE

A BLIZZARD

You're hiking over to a friend's house, when all of a sudden a surprise blizzard comes out of nowhere. Now that peaceful forest you were trekking through looks more like...well, you don't even know what because it's suddenly snowing so hard you can't see your frozen fingers in front of your face. Here's how to avoid becoming a permanent snowman:

HIDE.

Blizzard winds are so cold that they can cause immediate frostbite (talk about freezing your butt off!), and heavy, swirling snow can disorient you faster than a roomful of candy bars. If you're caught in a sudden storm, seek shelter immediately where you can stay warm and dry.

BUNDLE UP.

Better do this *before* you leave the house if the weather outside is frightful. Winter weather calls for loose-fitting, lightweight-but-warm layers that you can take off as you start to sweat. That goes double if you're surprised by a blizzard, when you'll want to make sure all your parts are covered up.

◉ Start with a thin T-shirt (don't worry, no one will see your old Bert and Ernie tee under all the other clothes) under a long-sleeve shirt under a sweater under a water-repellent coat.

◉ Wear two pairs of thick socks inside waterproof boots, opt for mittens instead of gloves, and wrap your face like a mummy with a scarf.

◉ And, yes, wear a hat. You'll have hat hair the rest of the day, but it's better than your strands breaking off like icicles.

BUILD A FORT.

If you can't find a nearby man-made shelter, start acting like a caveman and use what you have. Buffer yourself from wind by hunkering down near trees. Try to find long branches you can prop against a tree for a makeshift lean-to, and use snow for insulation. (Just keep the space small so you don't lose too much heat.) Huddling under a rock ledge can also provide some relief.

SNOWFLAKES GET SMALLER AS THE TEMPERATURE DROPS.

ALMOST 90 PERCENT OF SNOW IS AIR.

DON'T GET GROUNDED.

The bare frozen ground is no place for your keister. Pile leaves, twigs, grass, or other materials on the ground before sitting, unless you want to be stuck there till spring.

MAKE NEW BEST FRIENDS.

If you're stuck in a blizzard with someone, you're probably pretty good friends by now. Well, prepare to get even closer. If you're trapped outside with a bud, use each other's body heat to stay warm. Smoosh yourselves together, wrap your arms around each other, anything to transfer heat. Don't worry—no one will be around to take a picture and post it on Facebook.

AVOID FROZEN TREATS.

Don't eat the snow, no matter how hungry or thirsty you get. Chowing down on nature's snow cone will only lower your body temperature, which could lead to hypothermia, a life-threatening situation. Hopefully you told someone where you were going before you headed out, so rescuers will find you before you start hallucinating about giant talking glasses of water.

SNIRT IS SNOW COMBINED WITH DIRT.

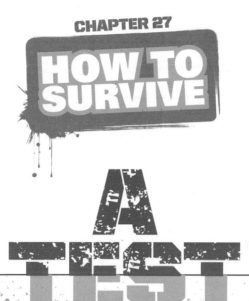

CHAPTER 27

HOW TO SURVIVE

A TEST

ow great would it be if all your tests looked like this?

1.   True or False: Ebenezer Scrooge was always a nice guy.

2.   Name one ingredient in peanut butter sandwiches.

3.   In 100 words, explain why you deserve a bigger allowance.

4.   Which of these is not in the United States: A. Texas; B. the Empire State Building; C. Mount Rushmore; D. the pyramids of Egypt.

Unfortunately for you, school tests are completely different. They're harder and more stressful. So it's OK—even normal—to get a little nervous before a test. But these tips will help you survive the hardest quiz, and maybe even take home an A.

MEMORIES—EVEN FACTS YOU'VE GONE OVER FOR A TEST—ARE STORED IN YOUR BRAIN WHILE YOU SLEEP.

DUH! STUDY!

Enough said. For study tips, check out the Supersmart Secrets sidebar.

SKIP THE LOCKER GOSSIP.

Get to class a little early so you don't feel rushed, which can stress you out. This also gives you a chance to go over the material one last time.

AVOID THE MUNCHIES.

Eat a good breakfast (or lunch, for afternoon tests). Healthy food will give you energy to focus. Plus, who wants to be distracted by your rumbling stomach?

GET SOME SHUT-EYE.

In scientific studies, students who lost sleep to cram for a test actually performed worse than students who got some zzz's. So don't hit the books for an all-nighter— hit the sack instead.

READ BEFORE YOU WRITE.

When your teacher first hands out the test; read it all the way through so you know what to expect. Then answer the easy questions first.

MAKE A BUDGET.

Spending the entire class writing out the Declaration of Independence when there are 19 other questions to answer is a one-way ticket to Flunksville. Figure out how much time you have to spend on each question, then stick to that plan.

PSYCH OUT THE TEST.

Obviously the way to ace a test is to understand the material. But if you get stuck, remember these secrets when taking a multiple-choice test:

◉ Read all the answers, get rid of the ones you know aren't correct, then make your choice.

◉ When "all of the above" or "none of the above" is an option on only a few questions, that might be your answer.

◉ If two answers are very similar except for a few words, one of those answers is probably correct.

◉ The answer with the most information is often the correct one.

◉ If you have a large number of choices for your answer, and you have no idea which is right, choose one of the two in the middle.

◉ Don't keep changing your answer. Your first response is often the correct one.

STUDIES HAVE SHOWN SOME KIDS MAY **ABSORB FALSE FACTS** FROM MULTIPLE-CHOICE TESTS.

HOW TO SURVIVE ANYTHING

TRUE, FALSE, OR MAYBE?

Try these hints for a True-or-False test:

◎ Usually more answers are true than false.

◎ Words like "always" and "never" can mean the statement is false.

◎ Words like "usually" and "sometimes" can mean the statement is true.

◎ If any part of the statement is false, then the answer is false.

◎ BUT, just because part of the statement is true doesn't mean that the *entire* statement is true.

FINISH IN SECOND PLACE.

Even if you finish your test early, don't immediately hand it over to the teacher. Instead, take some time to go back over your answers. That way, you can catch any really stupid mistakes you may have made (in this case it's OK to change your answer!), and you won't look like a dork trying to impress the teacher.

SUPERSMART SECRETS

Guess what? The best way to survive a test is to study for it. Here's how.

Start early. It's a lot easier to study 30 minutes a day the week before a test than three hours the night before. Block out some serious study time every day.

Be a copycat. No, we don't mean cheating off your BFF's paper. But if your teacher writes something on the board or repeats certain facts, it means it's important. Take down those notes (just don't forget where you put them) and review them before the test.

Be "memorable." Got a lot to memorize but have a horrible memory? Try making some flash cards. Write down the question on one side and the answer on the other.

Bookmark it. Reading about dead Presidents can be *soooo* boring—so boring that the minute you read it, you forget it. So take notes while you're reading. Jot down key dates and facts so you can review them later. (*Psst:* Just the act of writing down what you read helps you remember!)

Pretend you're a pilgrim. OK, we'll let you keep the lights on. But stay away from the TV, your iPod, instant messaging— anything that might distract you.

Give your brain a break. Most people can concentrate for about 45 minutes at a time. So give yourself 15 minutes every so often to talk on the phone, listen to a couple tunes, or read a magazine article.

CHAPTER 28

HOW TO SURVIVE

BEING ADRIFT AT SEA

I't's hard to imagine that the lazy day you've planned cruising the ocean on a boat will be anything less than relaxing. That is until your motor dies, you run out of gas, or your sail is in tatters. Now you're just drifting aimlessly on open waters, hoping someone will spot the little speck that is your boat. Here's how to deal until your rescue ship arrives.

GET A ROPE.

First, tie down everything you can. There's nothing worse than hitting a wave and watching your last granola bar become fish food.

POON LIM, A **CHINESE** SAILOR, SURVIVED 133 DAYS ALONE AT SEA FROM 1942-1943.

DRINK IT IN.

Forget becoming shark bait. Your biggest problem is having enough water. Start conserving what you have, and drink only a tiny bit during the first 24 hours. (Your body has what it needs for now.) After that, limit your intake to about 16 ounces (about the amount in two cans of soda) a day.

SAVE FOR A RAINY DAY.

Bottled water won't last forever, especially if you're halfway around the world by now. So gather up buckets, food containers, even snorkeling flippers to collect rainwater. You can also lick up dew or suck liquid out of a fish's eye. (Hey, it's better than cafeteria food.)

MAKE PALE THE NEW TAN.

Your goal that morning may have been to soak up some rays, but now the sun is your enemy. Avoid turning into a human lobster by covering up and staying in the shade (if you have it). Wear a hat and sunglasses, and use beach towels to wrap up exposed skin like a tortilla. Don't forget the tops of your feet, and, dude—wear sunscreen!

SOCK IT TO 'EM.

No sunglasses? No problem! Make two eye slits in a sock and tie it around your head. You'll look like a cool movie villain, and maybe the funky smell will lead rescuers right to you.

WATCH IT.

Create a schedule so that everyone onboard takes turns looking for rescuers. Just make sure whoever's up is looking for ships and airplanes—not daydreaming about ice-cream sundaes.

FOLLOW THAT BIRD.

Many seabirds hunt during the day and fly back to land at dusk. So toward sunset, let your new BFF (best feathered friend) use its all-natural GPS to lead you to dry ground.

MAKE AN EMERGENCY LANDING.

Land is better than water. If you spot it—even if it looks like a deserted island—try to steer your craft that way. (Aim for a nice soft beach rather than a bunch of rocks.) You're much easier to spot as a permanent fixture on a coastline than as a moving, might-as-well-be-a-fish dot on the open ocean.

THE OCEAN MAY LOOK LIKE ONE GIANT WATER COOLER. BUT THE SALT IN SEAWATER WILL ONLY DEHYDRATE YOU. SO DON'T DRINK IT!

BOAT-WORTHY

Whether you're water-skiing on a lake for an hour or doing an all-day ocean cruise, always make sure to have these things in your craft:

- Life jacket for every person
- Signaling device
- Water
- Rope or thick string
- Paddle or oar
- Sunscreen
- Jacket

HOW TO SURVIVE LIFE ON A DESERT ISLAND

Maybe that rescue boat or plane never came, but at least you've landed on a desert island. Congratulations! Now what?

QUENCH YOUR THIRST. Start digging a hole on the land side of a sand dune. Chances are freshwater is not too far below the surface. Plus, what else are you gonna do with your time?

OPEN A RESTAURANT. Your meals won't exactly be five-star-worthy, but they'll have to do. Look for plants that you know are edible and animals in shallow water and sand dunes. Seaweed may be your best friend: Small critters call it home, plus you can eat the greens like a salty, mushy salad.

BUILD A BEACHFRONT CONDO. Your I Love Grandma beach towel is not going to protect you from harsh sun, chilly nights, rain, or hungry insects looking for a feast.

◎ Unless you want your new vacation home washed out to sea, pick a spot for your shelter above the high-tide line (the highest point the water rises to on the beach during the day).

◎ Start building with your entrance facing north or south to keep those rays at bay. (Hint: The sun rises in the east and sets in the west.)

◎ If you washed ashore with a survival raft and tarp, it's your lucky day! Bury about a fifth of the raft in the sand so it stands straight up. Attach the tarp to the top and drape it to the ground, securing it with rocks or tree limbs.

◎ If you don't have a tarp, tip the raft a bit and prop it up with a paddle. You may have some furry friends come visit you at night, but at least you won't crisp up during the day.

◎ No trees on your island? Sit under anything that will keep you out of the sun—a cliff, a cave entrance, or whatever clothing you can spare.

◎ Gather leaves and grass to use as a bed. It won't be as comfortable as home, but at least you won't have to wash sand out of weird places.

BE A BEACHCOMBER. You never know what's going to wash up on shore. Keep your eyes open for lost cargo and garbage that you can recycle into survival gear. Collect sun-dried driftwood as well. It burns easily for cooking or signaling; it can also be used to build a shelter.

GO FISH. This may take some time, but that's one thing you've got a lot of. Use rope, string, or cloth to make a fishing line; a pop-top from a soda can will fill in as a hook.

GET CREATIVE. Use whatever you can find to survive. Shoelaces become fishing line. Shiny stuff becomes signaling mirrors. Metal objects become things to hunt, fish, cut, scrape, or puncture with.

CHAPTER 29

HOW TO SURVIVE

STRESSING OUT

We hear you. Just because you're not an adult doesn't mean you don't have stuff to stress out about. Pressures from teachers, homework, friends, sports, music class, extracurricular activities, volunteer commitments, and even your family can all add up. Before your head explodes, try these stay-sane tips.

DRAIN YOUR BRAIN.

Get your mind off things by doing something fun that will put you in a good mood. Go for a walk, ride your bike, listen to music, read a book, or play with your dog.

BREATHE.

It sounds ridiculous: Who would forget to breathe? But when things start to feel out of control, a few deep breaths will help calm you down. Inhale slowly and deeply through your nose, hold for a few seconds, then exhale through your mouth. Do this three or four times. (More than that and you might pass out. That may help your friends de-stress with all the laughing and pointing, but it'll do nothing for your own stress level.)

LAUGHTER HAS BEEN SCIENTIFICALLY PROVEN TO REDUCE STRESS.

TENSE UP.

If all you're thinking about as you're trying to fall asleep is how to answer the essay question "Why did Charles Dickens name his book *Great Expectations*?" try this relaxation technique. Tense the muscles in your feet for ten seconds, then relax. Now tense the muscles in your calves, then relax. Keep tensing your knees, thighs, hips, and all the way up your body until you feel one with the mattress. P.S. The correct answer is because *Good Expectations* wasn't impressive enough.

DISAPPOINT SOMEONE.

One reason you're so stressed is because you've got too much to do. Seriously. It's OK to ditch your friends if you need to be by yourself, turn down a babysitting job to study a little more, or quit one of your 18 gajillion extracurricular activities to concentrate on the 17 gajillion most important ones. Just let people know that you need some extra "me" time and they'll understand.

DREAM ON A FULL STOMACH.

Stress can totally mess with your body, so you need to make sure you're sleeping enough (at least nine hours) and eating healthy. (Potato chips and french fries do *not* count as veggies.) Your body needs zzzz's and grub to help it recover from the daily grind.

SHOCK YOUR PARENTS: THINK POSITIVE.

When you're stressed, it's easy to feel like you've fallen in a deep, dark pit and can't get out. But staying positive gives you energy to survive the toughest challenges. Instead of thinking you'll never get through that pile of homework, remind yourself how smart you'll be when you're done. Instead of dreading swim practice, think about how much faster you'll be able to get out of the water when a shark is spotted if you keep practicing.

TALK IT OUT.

What a shocker: Your friends are probably just as stressed out as you are. Take some time to complain, rant, yell—anything to get the stress out of your system. You'll feel better, plus your friend may have some good advice to give.

ACCEPT THE LOSER IN YOU.

News flash: You are not perfect. You are not going to get straight A's every single day, place first at every single event, catch every single ball that comes your way, know every single answer to your teacher's questions, and get your parents to agree with you every single time. Don't set unrealistic expectations for yourself; all anyone can do is his or her best.

TAKE CONTROL

One way to keep stress below the boiling point is to stay organized. Keep your life in control with these tips.

Make a to-do list. Write down everything you need to do that day in order of importance. (Hint: Walking your little sister home from school is at the top; updating your Facebook status is at the bottom.) Scratch things off your list as you accomplish them. It's OK to carry over tasks to the next day!

Keep a calendar. Mark down dates of big tests, major homework assignments, sports tournaments, and school plays. Also block out regular commitments, such as rehearsals, sports practices, or jobs like mowing lawns, as well as time every night for homework.

Break big projects into little chunks. Back in February you marked on your calendar that your science project is due April 15. Great. But unless your name is Albert Einstein the Third, you can't just wait to start the project on April 14. Give yourself due dates along the way for little goals: Come up with the idea by February 15. Do preliminary research by February 28. Conduct all tests by March 15. State your findings by April 1. Finesse your report by April 15. Receive an A+++ by April 22.

Prioritize. If you're feeling overwhelmed, make a list of all your activities. Figure out which ones are necessary (uh, homework), which ones are optional, and which of the latter are most important to you. Ditching just one will help you feel more in control.

Clean your room. OK, we won't go that far. But try to keep an organized study space. If you have a desk, keep pens, pencils, paper, staplers, calculators, etc. where you can find them. If you study at the kitchen table, keep a box of supplies handy so you're not wasting time searching for your fuzzy purple pen. Get rid of distractions like TV, music, and phones. The good news: This also includes your little brother. Here's your opportunity to get your parents to back you up so he leaves you alone.

Organize your locker. What's the point of frantically digging through gym shorts, wadded-up paper, gum wrappers, last week's bologna sandwich, and those forms you were supposed to take home for your dad to sign, just to find your Spanish book at the bottom of your locker ten minutes later? An organized locker is one less thing to stress out about, so give it a shot. At least for a week.

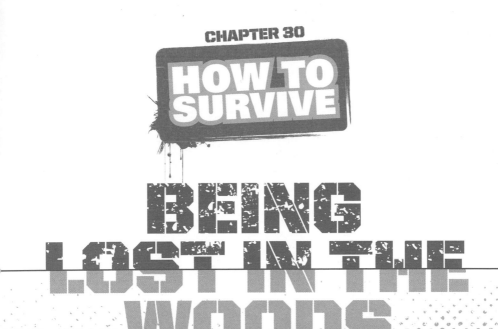

CHAPTER 30

HOW TO SURVIVE

BEING LOST IN THE WOODS

O K. Now that you've passed that tree that looks like your great-aunt Gertie for the fifth time, you can finally admit it: You're lost. Not lost like you're-never-gonna-figure-out-any-kind-of-math-problem-involving-two-trains lost. We're talking the-sun-is-going-down-over-a-never-ending-forest-and-even-your-dog-knows-you're-lost lost. Here's how to get found:

RELAX.

You told someone where you were going and what time you'd be back, right? So unless you spent the day before keying your dad's car or cutting up your mom's favorite dress with scissors, eventually someone's going to come looking for you.

HOW TO SURVIVE ANYTHING

ABOUT 30 PERCENT OF LAND ON THE GLOBE IS FOREST, BUT IT IS DISAPPEARING AT A RAPID RATE.

▶ FIND A HANGOUT.

Look for a place that can be seen from the air but still has some trees to protect you from the sun. Find a dry, flat spot near a water source—just not too close, unless your method of getting found is to get swept downstream to the ocean when a lake or river floods.

▶ STAY PUT.

It may be tempting to think, "This time I *know* I'm gonna be able to find my way out." But that's just going to get you more lost and make it difficult for rescuers to find you. So have a seat, count the birds, chew some gum, start writing that Grammy-winning song in your head, and just wait.

▶ QUENCH YOUR THIRST— CAREFULLY.

That river or stream may look like a big ice-cold glass of water, but to animals, it's a supersize toilet. Most freshwater sources will be contaminated with microorganisms, so if you didn't bring iodine or chlorine tablets to purify water, find another source. Collect rainwater or dew off plants instead.

REDECORATE.

Around your hangout, tie as many brightly colored things as you can find around trees to attract attention from rescuers both on the ground and in the air. Don't use your clothes— you'll need them to stay warm at night. Instead, use paper, hair ribbons, cloth from that teddy bear you secretly stashed in your backpack— anything that will get you noticed.

MAKE A SCENE.

Don't immediately start shouting for help when you first get lost. If you're really lost, only the birds will hear your cries, and you'll just lose your voice. Wait until you hear rescuers to start screaming like a banshee. If you hear a plane, don't chase it. Instead, get to a clearing, lie on the ground, and start moving like you're making a snow angel.

GIMME SHELTER!

Once you find a place to hang out for a while, try to make a shelter and a bed.

◉ Find a long, thick branch. Lean it against a tree on a lower branch.

◉ Gather lots of leafy branches, and prop them against the leaning branch. The enclosure should be just big enough for you. Any bigger and you'll be roomies with the cold air.

◉ Fill in exposed parts with leaves, mud, and moss. Now you have a wall to protect you from rain and wind.

◉ The bare ground gets cold at night, so make a "mattress" to keep you from literally chillin'. Stack moss, leaves, and branches as thick as your mattress at home. Pile leaves and moss on top of you to create a "blanket."

THE WILD LIFE

When you're lost and a little scared, any noise can sound like Bigfoot coming after you—even though it's most likely a squirrel or a mouse. Still, you could find yourself trying to explain to a grumpy bear or moose why you're in its front yard. Here's how to survive.

BEAR

Write this down: You cannot outrun or outfight a bear. Avoid crossing paths with one in the first place by making lots of noise when hiking—singing, jangling your keys, whatever—and by not leaving food scraps or garbage near you. Don't keep food in your shelter, and if, uh, nature calls, answer it away from your campsite, since the odor may attract a curious bear.

Grizzlies live in the northern United States (including Alaska) and Canada. Your best defense against one of these guys is to play dead: Lie flat on your tummy, interlace your fingers on top of your neck, and pray it goes away. If it rolls you on your back, keep rolling until you're back on your belly.

Black bears are much more common than grizzlies and live all over the United States and in Asia. They won't stop attacking a fake-dead hiker, so fight back. Hit its snout or eyes with a rock or a stick (or anything you have) to convince it that maybe it'd be happier attacking something else.

MOOSE

That's right. Moose (or European Elk as it's called in Europe). This isn't your dad's goofy Bullwinkle cartoon character. This is the largest member of the deer family, with sharp antlers to stick you with and powerful legs to kick your stomach out your back and stomp you into the ground.

A moose will not try to eat you, but it will attack if it feels threatened. If you come across one and it hasn't noticed you, don't approach it. If it does check you out, speak to it like you're trying to soothe a tantrum-throwing two-year-old and slowly back away.

If you're charged by a moose, run like you're Frankenstein being chased by an angry mob (just run faster than the movie monster). Most likely the moose just wants you out of its territory and won't chase you far. As a last resort, make like a squirrel and scramble up a tree.

Too slow? If you're knocked down, curl up like a ball and hope the moose doesn't want to play soccer. Protect your head. Do not move.

169

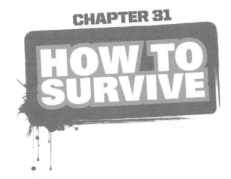

CHAPTER 31

HOW TO SURVIVE

A BREAKUP

Do you still make mudpies like you did when you were three? Do you ever pull out your little toy soldiers and play war like you did when you were seven? Didn't think so. People change as they get older. And sometimes, people change so much that they don't want to be friends or boyfriend-girlfriend anymore. If you're the one being dumped, it sucks. Big-time. Read on to learn how to get through it.

CONTROL THE INSANITY.

Breaking up can feel like you've been kicked in the gut by a horse. But stay calm. Don't cry, yell, or insult the other person. That just makes you look like a loser and gives the other person more confidence that the decision to steer clear of you was the right one.

DON'T BE A DOORMAT.

It's OK to ask for an explanation why this person doesn't want to hang around with you anymore as long as you can take the truth—and as long as the other person wants to talk. Understand that even though you're dying to know if it was your new faux hawk that scared off your crush, she may want to just move on. If you do score a meeting, remember that calm is key. No one wants to explain anything to someone who's acting like they need to be wearing a straitjacket.

NOW YOU CAN CRY LIKE A BABY.

Still, it's OK to be sad—after all, you've lost someone important to you. Give yourself space to listen to some sad tunes, take a walk by yourself, or just stare at the wall. At least your parents will appreciate the quiet.

DON'T BLAME YOURSELF.

Your friend or crush may not have seen all the good things about you, but that doesn't mean that you aren't awesome. Remind yourself of how smart you are in math, how great your hair looks, or how well you can play the piano. Your friend or crush may not have appreciated those things—but other people will.

DITCH THE BLACK CAPE, TOP HAT, AND FAKE MUSTACHE.

If someone doesn't want to hang out with you anymore, that's her problem. But don't make things worse by starting rumors that the person still wets the bed or gossiping about his fear of spiders. That just shows that you care too much about what the other person thinks. Don't waste a second of your newfound independence trying to take revenge.

LEAVE THE STALKING FOR CELEBRITIES.

So someone doesn't want to be friends anymore. Whatever. Don't become his own personal stalker by accidentally-on-purpose running into him or checking his tweets every ten minutes. He's moving on. You should, too.

STAND YOUR GROUND.

When you get dumped, your first instinct may be to lock yourself in the bathroom for three days or start wearing a bag over your head. Don't. Even if the other person is on the swim team with you, or sits with the same group of friends at lunch, stay put. Don't change your life to avoid seeing this person. You have as much right to be there as anyone else.

FIND THE FUN.

It's OK to give yourself time to mope, but then go have some fun. See a movie, bike with some friends, or just hang out with your family. (See? They *are* good for something!)

HOW TO BE A
GOOD BREAKER-UPPER

No one wants to be rejected. So if you're the one doing the dumping, try to make it a little less painful for the other person.

◎ Figure out why you want to end things. Is it because your BFF keeps spilling your secrets? Or because your crush refuses to hang out with your friends? Understand what the problem is so you can clearly communicate it.

◎ Practice what you're going to say. Use a mirror or another friend.

◎ Have the conversation face-to-face, or at least on the phone. Don't dump via email, text message, IM, or Facebook.

◎ On the bus or at lunch surrounded by loads of people is not the right place to have this talk. Choose a quiet location without a lot of curious ears.

◎ Don't make the other person feel at fault. Use "I" phrases like "I want to spend more time with my other friends," or "I don't like feeling that I can't tell you things."

◎ Listen to what the other person has to say. It's OK if she gets angry and vents—that's normal. But if you start to feel uncomfortable or unsafe, leave.

◎ Don't change your mind. Before you have this conversation, make sure that this is the absolute, 100 percent, no-second-thoughts right decision, then stick to it. Having to do this all over again isn't anybody's idea of a good time.

◎ Be cool. There's no need to make dumpees feel even worse by talking about them behind their backs, laughing at them in the hallways, or ignoring them in class.

C U L8R
WHEN YOUR BEST FRIEND MOVES AWAY

You can tell yourself that you'll be friends forever, but when one friend moves away, it doesn't always work out that way. It's almost impossible to keep the friendship from changing, but that doesn't mean things have to go the way of the dinosaurs. Here's how to make the most of a long-distance friendship.

Figure out the best way to stay in touch: phone, Skype, IMs, or even snail mail. Just make sure you get everyone's parents' OK first.

Set a time to chat. You probably can't talk every day, but scheduling an every-Saturday-at-10 gabfest helps you keep in touch and gives you something to look forward to.

Make some memories. Before your friend leaves, make two scrapbooks—one for you and one for your BFF—to remember all the fun you've had. Other ideas could include: a video of all your favorite places, a playlist of your favorite songs, or just a card signed by all your friends.

Beware the green monster. Accept that your BFF will have to make new friends to survive at a new school, so don't be jealous of them.

Don't feel guilty if you find a new friend. Nothing will ever replace your old BFF and the times you've shared, but it's OK to expand your friend circle.

AFTERWORD

So now that you've read every page of this book, you are totally prepared to face any obstacle. . . . right? Well, not exactly. But you might be better off than most.

Here's a secret that most old people don't have the heart to tell you: Life is hard. No matter what you do, or how well you prepare, you're always going to face some unexpected challenges that make cyberbullies seem friendly and rattlesnakes look like kitty cats. But here's another secret: It's how you deal with these obstacles that make you who you are.

So go out and live your life. Don't be afraid of the unexpected. After all, the more challenges you face, the easier it gets. . . . because once you stare in the face of an angry grizzly, maybe you'll realize your mean math teacher isn't so bad after all. . . .

Then again, if your math teacher brings her pet lion to administer a pop quiz in the middle of a blizzard with a tornado barreling down on you—you're on your own.